THE ART OF PROFESSIONAL COMMUNICATION

PIYUSH B. CHAUDHARY

THE ART OF PROFESSIONAL COMMUNICATION

STRATEGIES FOR SUCCESS IN PROFESSIONAL LIFE

PIYUSH B. CHAUDHARY

ASSISTANT PROFESSOR
DEPARTMENT OF ENGLISH
HANS RAJ COLLEGE, UNIVERSITY OF DELHI

KALAMOS LITERARY SERVICES LLP

Kalamos Literary Services LLP
Email: info@kalamos.co.in | editorial@kalamos.co.in
First Published in 2024 by

Kalamos Literary Services

ISBN- 978-81-19601-43-1
Copyright © *Piyush B. Chaudhary* (2024)

The Art of Professional Communication: Strategies for Success in Professional Life
Piyush B. Chaudhary

Cover Designed & Typeset in Kalamos Literary Services LLP

Print and bound in India.

Contents

PREFACE

Welcome to the transformative journey of mastering professional communication. In today's dynamic and interconnected world, the ability to communicate effectively is not merely a skill but a vital asset that distinguishes successful professionals from unsuccessful ones.

The book was 4 years in the making. The idea for this book was first conceived during the Covid-19 pandemic and the subsequent need to adapt to changing demands in the education sector. A lot of the material I have used in this book was first prepared, in rough drafts, to share with students at University of Delhi, during the turbulent times that 2020 presented us with. What started as brief handouts for my students has today taken up the form of a full-fledged book. I could not have been happier to see the project turning to fruition after more than 4 years. I dedicate the book to the readers as one of the motivating factors behind this book was to allow ideas to grow, somewhat similar to what Oliver W. Holmes famously said: "Many ideas grow better when transplanted into another mind than the one where they sprang up". I therefore, dedicate this book to the students of communication and to the general readers, the fountainhead of my inspiration.

Whether you are a seasoned professional looking to refine your skills or a student eager to grasp the fundamentals, this book aims to equip you with the necessary tools and insights. The book is primarily aimed for undergraduate students across the various universities in India which are now following the NEP-2020 framework. The NEP-2020 clearly holds communication skill as one of the most important life-skills in the 21st century. It aims at a free flow of pedagogical framework and aims for a smooth transition from School to University and beyond. The book therefore, is curated keeping in mind this transitional approach which aligns itself with the guiding principles of NEP-2020 and yet is a useful and practical addition for a general reader too. Skill development is a facet embedded in the NEP-2020 and it envisages imparting professional skills to students as part of their holistic education. This is also enshrined in the UGCF-2022 framework adopted at the University of Delhi. As part of UGCF-2022, students at the University of Delhi are required to study a Skill Enhancement Course (SEC) as part of their undergraduate degree. This book is closely and accurately aligned with the SEC syllabi offered in DU & taught by English departments across the University. UGCF, modelled on NEP is a democratic step, a break from earlier modes of education towards a more student centric, multidisciplinary, research-oriented, skill-based & holistic curriculum aimed at breaking new grounds & preparing the incoming generations to be academically & professionally prepared for their lives ahead. This book is just an attempt in that direction. The book will surely be useful in other central universities as well, implementing the NEP-2020.

As India strives to be a developed state, it is imperative that the youth excel in communication skills. The book is aimed keeping in mind the immediate and significant communication skills that any graduate or job-seeker can hone and utilise within the larger professional space. As an undergraduate student embarking on your academic journey, you are on the threshold of discovering the critical role that effective communication plays in your future career success. Whether you aspire to enter the realms of business, engineering, healthcare, academia, public sector or private sector, mastering professional communication skills will be essential in distinguishing yourself as a competent and confident professional.

This book, crafted by years of teaching and research in the field of communication, aims to equip you with the tools, insights, and strategies necessary to excel in diverse professional contexts. This book is designed to be your comprehensive guide in navigating the intricate landscape of communication in professional settings. This book is structured to be your comprehensive companion on your journey to mastering professional communication. Each chapter is meticulously crafted to address key aspects of communication essential for success in today's workplace. I have tried to incorporate practical advice, real-world examples, and actionable strategies to enhance the professional prowess of young aspirants, thereby enhancing the practical relevance of this book.

Moreover, this book delves into the complexities of communication beyond mere technique. It explores the importance of emotional intelligence, cultural sensitivity, and ethical considerations in fostering meaningful and impactful communication. In an era where global interconnectedness and diversity are the norms, understanding how to communicate respectfully and effectively across cultures and contexts is not just advantageous but imperative. Perhaps this is one of the key aspects which distinguishes a prospective job candidate from others.

The future belongs to the corporate sector and in such a scenario it is most imperative to have strong communication skills which one can apply in their professional life. Communication is at the heart of every human interaction, and its impact extends far beyond the exchange of words. Effective communication is not just a skill; it is the cornerstone of success in any professional endeavour. As a professor of Literature & Communication, I have witnessed firsthand, how adept communication can foster collaboration, drive innovation, and elevate individuals and organizations to new heights of success. I have witnessed firsthand, the transformative power of clear, concise, and strategic communication. It can build bridges, forge alliances, and propel careers forward. Conversely, I have seen how miscommunication or a lack of clarity can lead to misunderstandings, conflict, and missed opportunities.

As you embark on this journey, I encourage you to approach each chapter with curiosity and a willingness to learn. Reflect on your own communication strengths and areas for growth, challenge yourself to implement new strategies, and consider how the strategies and principles outlined in this book can be applied to your professional endeavours. Whether you are preparing for a job interview, negotiating a business deal, or simply striving to communicate more effectively with colleagues, the principles outlined here will prove to be your indispensable companion.

I am deeply grateful for the opportunity to share my insights and knowledge with you through this book. We hope that it will serve as a practical and inspirational guide, empowering the readers to communicate with confidence, clarity, and authenticity in all professional interactions.

Thank you for choosing this book as your companion on the path to mastering professional communication. Here's to your continued growth and success.

- Piyush B. Chaudhary

Unit 1
Professional Communication – Theory & Basics

Learning Objectives

In this unit we will learn about the basic concepts of communication as a subject. Communication is a process so central to human lives that it has been studied by multiple scholars. This unit will help you gain an in-depth understanding of the communication process, the major components it includes, and how they work together in the communication cycle. Students will learn to understand the significance of communication in professional life and gain insights to understand it better as a subject. This section also brings you the major models and theories of communication which help us look at the concept of communication with various theoretical perspectives. These theoretical perspectives are important to see the development of the concept of communication over a period of time.

This section further explains the major types of communication and how they can be used through various examples. In order to master communication skills, it is important to understand the factors to make it efficient. A significant part of your communication efficiency lies in the absence of communication barriers. This part of the book focuses on understanding communication barriers which occur in various situations and how to deal with them to minimize miscommunication and maximise effective communication. This unit provides a clear, concise and in-depth understanding of various concepts of communication along with practical examples to ace communication skills in your professional life.

Introduction

Humans are social beings and it is impossible for us to survive in isolation. The larger society is created by us as its parts in unity. We rely on each other in order to sustain our lives personally, professionally, socially, academically, and financially. For this purpose, we communicate with each other in order to convey our messages and information. This process is known as communication.

Communication is known as a natural process that has the purpose of carrying and conveying emotions, thoughts, feelings, ideas and information among human beings. This is done through the use of words, symbols, signs and movement of the body which is also known as body language. Communication is a significant activity which is needed in order to survive. It is not possible without the transmission of information and connecting with each other. It is an essential process which occurs everywhere humans exist. Every human takes a part in the process of communication with or without their intentions. From a baby crying for milk to an adult communicating about their different types of needs, are all the examples of communication. Communication is an indiscernible part of every interaction we take part in and human life as a whole. However, it is important to understand that communication is an activity rooted in the social sphere firstly. It is known as one of the most important conditions that make interaction socially possible which is the most basic foundation of the life of humans as social beings. For the sustainability of human life communication is needed in everyday life for us to be able to share, understand and receive information from other humans and make use of it.

What is Communication?

The word communication has come from the Latin word *Communis*. It means 'common'. The process of conveying information, opinions, facts, ideas and emotions by using the form of signs, words, symbols, signals and the movement of the body or gestures is known as communication. This process of communication helps in establishing a sense of commonness among people. Keith Davis gives the definition of communication as, "communication is the transfer of information and understanding from one person to another", in his book *Human Behaviour at Work*.

The process of communication happens when information, understanding and knowledge are being transferred by someone to someone else. The involvement of at least two people or parties is important for this process to take place. A message or a piece of information is transmitted by one party and this message is received and understood by the other party as per its meaning that was intended by the party that transmitted this message. One of these parties or both of these parties can be humans or they can be non human beings as well as non living objects. For instance, when a message is conveyed by a human to an animal, and the feelings of the animal are conveyed to the person by the animal. In another way which is similar to this example, a message is conveyed by the poster it is printed on. That too is also communication.

From the descriptions given above, communication can be taken as the act of information, feelings, thoughts, ideas and knowledge being transmitted at a one-sided level by an individual to another individual or a group of individuals. But communication is not limited to this transmission of a message as a one-way process. Communication is a two-sided engagement which includes not just the act of a message being sent but also the process of the message being received. That is why communication can be known as the process of information, ideas, feelings, and emotions being shared or exchanged among two or more parties. The equal participation of the party who sends the message and the party who receives the message is needed in the process of communication. The message is conveyed to the receiver by the side of the sender, and the feedback of the message is conveyed to the sender by the receiver of the message, in return. This process can be seen as an intercourse of information with the use of signs, symbols, signals and words. This process takes place to establish a mutual understanding.

Communication is one of the most essential parts of human life. From the beginning of our day to the end of it there are hundreds of moments when we communicate. Communication is significant in order to express our thoughts and ideas and to understand others' thoughts and ideas. Everything that includes more than a single person is dependent on communication. From the major events of one's professional life like cracking a job interview to everyday activities in one's work space like explaining your ideas to your boss and planning with your team, and to the most crucial aspects of one's personal life like from being able to understand the level of compatibility with a partner in order to decide the future of your relationship, to everyday things like expressing your emotions to your friends and family and understanding their emotions and needs - all depend on communication. Hence, communication is like a thread that connects you to the world around you. It is only through the act of communication we can sustain our relationships and fulfil our daily needs. The importance of communication in both every day and professional life lies in its ability to make us understand and connect with others. Improving your communication skills is important not just to excel in your professional life but it is also important to make your everyday life better. In order to improve one's communication skills it is important to understand that nobody is born as a master of communication. From our birth we keep learning the art of communication throughout our lives. So, it is possible for everyone to get better at communication and with understanding the process of communication and how it works along with practicing communication with the right tools. Anyone can master the art of communication and become excellent in communication which ultimately plays a significant role in your professional as well as personal success.

Significance of Communication

Communication is a significant part of our daily life. It is helpful in allowing people to create relations that are meaningful. The conversations we have with our friends, family, teachers, classmates and others are some of the most common examples of communication and it shows how much significance communication holds in our everyday life. Most of the time we practice communication through speaking, writing or using a similar type of signs or symbols but sometimes we practice communication with the use of our body movement as well. In order for our needs to be met communication is important. It is one of the most crucial parts when it comes to one's success in personal as well as professional spheres of their life.

The role that communication plays is significant and important to improve one's personal as well as professional life. Organizations share, distribute and disseminate information among them. The survival of any organization largely depends on its communication network. It is only possible through communication that the organizations are able to put their agenda or goal forward and make strategies to achieve their goals. Communication creates a sense of connection among employees that helps them work better towards a sharer goal. The importance of communication is not limited to helping organizations work more effectively but it also allows the organizations to get connected to the people externally like their customers, government, and suppliers etc, and it opens up the door of more and better opportunities.

With globalization organizations have started to have their businesses in multiple companies. In order to run their businesses smoothly organizations need the network of effective communication established within the organizations and among its employees as well as externally with its customers, suppliers and other partners. This process cannot be possible without communication.

The discussion that is given above provides us the insights in helping us to understand the significance of communication in all spheres of our life from personal to professional. The importance of communication is not limited to any one aspect of our life but it is essential for everything in our life.

> "The most important thing in communication is hearing what isn't said."
> -Peter Drucker

Communication Cycle/ Process of Communication

The cycle of the process of a message or the messages being transmitted and received is known as the communication cycle. This is a social interaction and it requires the involvement of at least two parties that need to interact with each other. One of these two parties can be a person, and at the place of the other party, there can be a human too or a non-human, non-living object as well. The message is communicated by one of these two parties, and it is received and understood by the other party as per its meaning intended by the party which sent this message. In order for the receiver to understand the meaning of the message that is being communicated, the involvement of the process of selecting, producing and transmitting signs and symbols is needed. This is called the cycle of communication.

This cycle includes the following elements:

1. Sender

The source of a message being transmitted for a certain purpose is known as the sender. The sender is also known as a transmitter. The cycle of communication has its beginning when a thought or idea comes to the mind of the sender which they wish to get conveyed to the other person with the purpose to achieve a certain goal. This process begins with the sender formulating an idea clearly in their mind about the message. The message is shaped by the logical faculty of the sender as well as by their mental attitude. The idea is encoded and translated into the symbols that are transmittable in nature. The symbols, time and channel to send the message are decided by its sender. This whole cycle of communication begins with the sender and it ends when the feedback of the message is comprehended by the sender. There are multiple examples of what a sender is. They can be a writer, a speaker or a teacher or an actor. For instance, the speaker in a class would be the teacher who is teaching there. The cycle of communication is started by the sender and the message gets communicated by the sender that is why the sender is also called the communicator. It is not necessary for the sender to be a human being; the sender can be a non-human or non-living object as well.

2. Message

The information that is conveyed by the sender is known as the message. A message can include an emotion, idea, thought or opinion. A message can be conveyed verbally, in a written or oral form and it can also be conveyed in non- verbal form which means without using words. The message is present in the mind of the sender. A message must have these significant characteristics like it should be well organized, properly structured, well-shaped and selective in nature. For instance, a topic that the teacher has taught is an example of a message. Without a message being in existence, communication cannot be possible. It is important for the message to be properly crafted, it should be clear and complete, without lacking any significant information. And it should be unambiguous as well.

3. Encoding

The process in which the information or data is converted into codes is known as encoding. It includes the process of the message being translated into symbols. These symbols can be in multiple forms like action, words, pictures, audio or signs and signals and in audio-visual form as well. The mind of the sender is the place where this process takes place. The thoughts of the sender need to be put in a form that can be understood by others. The sender can use many forms to convey their message such as signs, actions, symbols and words, gestures or even pictures as well. This is an important step that allows your message to be understood by others. The selection of the symbols by the sender depends on the kind of message they intend to send and on the ability of understanding and interpreting of the receiver so the message can be understood in the correct manner. This type of method helps in having a structure to the message. It is possible through the use of a communication medium. This medium can be verbal or non-verbal. For instance, the topic that needs to be taught in the class is prepared by the teacher and the way of teaching the topic is also decided by the teacher, whether the teaching should be through lectures or visuals. So, the symbols of the message are translated into the minds of the teacher while reading the lesson.

4. Channel

The path that is used for the message being passed is known as the channel. The sender and receiver are connected through the channel. Two of the significant channels of communication are known to be sight and air. The selection of the channel should be made by the sender while having the receiver kept in their minds. This choice of selecting the channel is also dependent on which type of message is being sent and on what type of relationship the sender and the receiver have with each other. If the relationship between the sender and the receiver is informal then the sender should choose the channel that is informal. But if it is the case of communicating as an organization, then it is important for the sender to choose the channel that is formal. In a similar manner, the channel can be chosen as an informal one if its nature is informal. And the channel should be formal if the nature of the message is formal as well.

It is important to understand that the channel and the medium are two different things. The channel can be understood as the path by which a message is passed. While on the other hand, medium is known as the message's carrier. For instance, when it comes to communicating orally, air is seen as the channel while voice is what we can call as the medium. In a similar manner, a letter is seen as the medium of the message while the channel is in the form of postal or courier service. The role that is played by the medium is significant in delivering the message. If the medium is inappropriate, it can cause huge harm to the goal of communication.

5. Receiver

The party that the message is directed to and who receives the message is known as the receiver. It is not necessary for the receiver to be a human being; it can be a non-human or non-living object. The receiver serves the purpose of receiving the message, decoding it, and understanding its meaning as it was intended by the sender and conveying the feedback to the sender. The receiver is known as the destination of the message. The receiver is always situated at the receiving end of the whole communication process. The major function of the receiver includes receiving and decoding the message that has been communicated in the form of words, signs and symbols, and drawing meaning from the message. This is the reason why the receiver can also be called a "decoder". The receiver can be anyone who receives a message, like a listener, viewer or a reader. For instance, in a classroom setting, the students can be seen as the receiver. Without the presence of a receiver, the cycle of communication cannot be complete.

6. Decoding

The process of interpreting the message meaningfully is known as decoding. Decoding is very different from encoding; it can be seen opposite to it. It can be explained as an act that allows the codes to get translated into meaningful information. The receiver performs this act and this act happens in the mind of the receiver. It is helpful in interpreting the meaning of the message for the receiver. This process can be seen as a mental process where the meaning of a message is drawn by the receiver through signs, symbols, words and pictures. These symbols are translated meaningfully into a message that now has a meaning and can be understood. For instance, students listening to their class and drawing meaning from the information that is being communicated through signs, symbols, words and signals.

7. Feedback

Feedback stands for the receiver's response or their reply to the message that is sent by the sender. It also works as a confirmation that the message has been received by the receiver. Feedback is intended for the sender and this is the final step of the communication cycle. For example, after a lecture the responses of the students can be seen as the feedback to the teacher.

> "How well we communicate is not determined by how well we say things but how well we are understood."
> -Andrew Grove

Significance of Feedback

Feedback is one of the most significant parts of the communication process. The roles of the sender and the receiver can be reversed and reciprocated. Feedback allows the receiver to turn into a sender and the sender into a receiver.

Feedback is an important tool that is helpful in measuring how effective communication is. The sender can rely on feedback by the receiver to make sure that the message that they sent has been understood clearly. It helps the sender improve their style of communication. The sender should try to understand through the feedback if the message was understood by the receiver in the way that was intended, or if there are some corrections or improvements that are needed to be made by the sender. The process of feedback is particularly important for allowing the receiver to raise questions and clear any doubt that might occur regarding the message. It also helps in boosting confidence.

The ultimate purpose of communication is to understand. But it is important to understand that understanding does not mean that there should be agreement. If the message was not understood by the receiver in a clear manner, then their feedback would be negative; and in case of the message getting understood by the receiver completely then it would result into an affirmative feedback from the receiver. So, the bottom line is that feedback depends on the receiver and how they perceive the message. It can be positive as well as negative. Feedback is an essential part of the communication process. Feedback can be in multiple forms, for example, verbal and non-verbal or even in the form of facial expressions like, smile, nod and sighs, and through our body language as well.

There are some major advantages of Feedback-

1. Feedback gives the confirmation that the message that was sent, has been received by the receiver.

2. It allows the listener or the receiver to clear their doubts if they have any.

3. It allows the sender to have insights about the interest of the sender.

4. It provides the sender an opportunity to correct or make the changes that are needed on the basis of feedback.

5. Feedback creates a sense of mutual connection between sender and the receiver that encourages communicating interactively.

6. Feedback is the last and the final part of the cycle of communication. The cycle of communication is completed with it.

Theory of Communication

Communication as a concept has been theorized by multiple theorists. The theory of communication provides us an analytical perspective on the major components, process and purpose of communication. Various theories explain the factors which are detrimental to understanding the ways to make communication efficient. These factors help us gain a logical understanding of the entire communication process and increase efficiency in our communication. Here are some of the major theories of communication:

Shannon-Weaver Model (1949)

This model of communication highlights the transmission of information, beginning with a sender and ending with a receiver. This model is highly used and theorized because it incorporates the major components of the communication process. These are the major components it includes:

a) **Sender**- communication process begins with it. It is the one who sends information known as a message.

b) **Encoder**- the way through which a message transmits is known as encoder. This includes various types of signals.

c) **Channel**- it is the medium which carries the message from the sender to the receiver.

d) **Decoder**- as the name suggests, it stands for the interpretation of the message at the receiver's end.

e) **Receiver**- it is the one who receives the message, the entity which the sender wanted to communicate the information to is known as a receiver.

Schramm's Model (1954)

This model challenges other models which perceive communication as a one-way process. It looks at it as a two way process which includes the reception of a message by the receiver and then sending a response to it as well.

Transactional Analysis by Eric Berne (1950s)

It is based on the role relationships play in communication. It takes into consideration experience and how the communication and relationships are affected by each other.

Berlo's SMCR Model (1960)

This model is focussed on the efficiency of the communication process. The term SMCR stands for:

a) **Source-** the one who sends the message.

b) **Message-** the information which the source communicates.

c) **Channel-** the device or the way which is used to transmit a message. It is the carrier of the message.

d) **Receiver-** the one by whom the message is received and decoded.

Diffusion of Innovation by Everret Rogers (1962)

This theory looks at the circulation of ideas and technology. It takes into consideration the role of culture in the spread of information. It emphasizes on social systems and how channels of communication work through them.

The Transactional Model of Communication (1967)

Developed by Barlund, in this model the focus is given on seeing the process of communication as an interaction between two parties. This model is circular in its structure and takes into consideration how communication occurs in real time.

The Cooperative Principle by Paul Grice (1975)

This model focuses on the idea of understanding and cooperation between the two parties. Communication takes place. It used the idea of maxims in communication to denote effectiveness of communication.

Types of Communication

There are three types of communications:

1. **Verbal communication**
2. **Written Communication**
3. **Non-Verbal communication**

Communication is divided into multiple types majorly based on the use of medium through which we decide to communicate our messages. These different types of communication help us choose a medium to share information which is most suitable and easily accessible to us in a certain situation. These multiple types of communication also help us decide the right way to communicate on a particular message.

1.   Verbal Communication

Verbal communication stands for the exchange of ideas through the use of structured language. It is the most commonly used type of communication. In professional life, most of the sorts of communication are verbal. It is suitable to express deep, critical and complex ideas and information. It is used to convey one's feelings and emotions as well in the proper way. There is a sense of rationality associated with verbal communication which makes it the best to use in formal and professional settings. It can take place orally and in a written manner as well.

Example:

- Speech spoken by a leader, phone call
- Newspaper, diary writing

2.   Written Communication

The communication that occurs with the use of writing words is known as written communication. It is in contrast to oral communication. Written communication is formal and helps us keep a record of things. Most of the correspondence in a professional setting is written. Written communication can be handwritten as well as digital. It is most useful for all types of professional, legal and administrative work where it is crucial to keep a record of communication. It is also useful to keep reminders and it helps to keep a note of things to revisit later.

Example:

- Report, memo, a letter to a friend
- Email, text message, online articles

3.   Non-Verbal Communication

Non-verbal communication is communication without the use of words. It does not include any kind of use of words, neither spoken nor written. There is a misconception that most of the communication we do is through words. But in reality, we communicate in many ways even when we are not speaking or writing anything. Most of the times, we neglect non-verbal clues which consist of much important information. Non-verbal language includes various audio and visual signs, body language, facial expressions, tone and pitch of voice, paralanguage, gestures, and sounds, to name a few. We can understand and gather a great deal of information from a person even if they are not speaking only if we pay attention to their non-verbal communication clues.

Example:

- Sound of scream or a cry
- Smile, handshake, emoticons used in online communication, or facial expressions

> "Nonverbal communication forms a social language that is in many ways richer and more fundamental than our words."
> -Leonard Mlodinow

Language of Communication

Language of professional communication can be either verbal or non-verbal communication. In a professional setting, both are equally important. In this section we will be focussing on the non-verbal aspects like body language, paralanguage, kinesics, proxemics, haptics, etc. Verbal language of professional communication will be dealt with later on in this book in the subsequent chapters. To put it broadly, the verbal language of communication will contain aspects based on speech and writing. The later parts of the book will be discussing these aspects of communication at length.

Non-Verbal Language

It can be easily argued that non-verbal language is used more than verbal language. In any professional setting, non-verbal language is equally important as it gives us the edge, the leadership skills required in any professional setting.

It includes:

Body Language

According to Allan and Barbara Pease, Body Language is nothing but an outward reflection of a person's emotional condition. And all these reflections can be clubbed under non-verbal language of communication.

Body language is a non-verbal mode of communication as it is not said or spoken directly. It may include gestures, grins, postures or expressions. The head of a person, their eyes, face, posture, gestures, clothing, appearances are all different elements of body language. It is with the head of a person that we judge whether they are submissive or aggressive. How one controls their eyes also speaks a lot about a person. Eye contact reflects a person's anxiety levels too. A very short eye contact, for instance, may represent nervousness or disinterest.

Similarly, our gestures and posture while communicating also shows a lot about our personality. Even hand gestures speak a lot about a person's thoughts. Hands deep in pocket can show unwillingness to engage in any conversation for any reason. Open hands and showing hands while speaking show a more reliable character and is a sign of openness. Politicians, public speakers use the open hand and open palm gesture to connect with the audience. This gesture shows trust and an honest approach.

Similarly, a cross armed posture may show submissiveness or disagreement. Clenched fists in a cross-armed posture can also show a hostile attitude of the person. Body language should be always seen in clusters and not in isolation. It can be learnt over a period of time and can be both understood and perfected by constant effort.

Paralanguage

The word para means 'similar to' or 'like' or 'supplement to'. Therefore, the word Paralanguage means like language but not exactly language. It is very close to language but is not exactly language. It is basically a middle path between verbal and non-verbal communication.

Paralanguage is a mode of non-verbal communication but it is extremely important in any form of communication. So, the tone of the words, loudness, softness, tone of the sentence, pitch, volume, etc is what comprises paralanguage. For e.g., the stress that we place on any particular word or phrase while we speak is part of paralanguage. Then intonation too plays an important role. Intonation is the pitch of the sentence. High pitch and low pitch denote different meanings while communicating. All these aspects make communication more effective. Basically, it completes the communication. Paralanguage makes communication more lively and effective. Therefore, Paralanguage may not be a part of verbal communication but it is still very important.

Barriers to Communication

What is a barrier? Anything that hinders, stops, impedes communication is a barrier. It is basically an obstacle, a hurdle, or a hindrance. What it does is that it slows down the communication and sometimes even stops it completely. In short, barriers to communication are certain situations which prevent smooth communication from taking place.

Some of the various barriers can be:
1. Physical Barriers
2. Psychological Barriers
3. Cultural Barriers

Let us try to understand each and every kind of barrier in greater detail and see how it prevents communication and leads to miscommunication at the both the general and at the professional levels.

Physical Barriers

a. Noise: It is the physical sound which can disrupt communication. For instance, too much noise in a gathering, faulty network while on call, excessively loud music in a social gathering, mechanical issues in any device, distance between the sender and receiver, adverse weather conditions, etc are some examples of noise acting as physical barriers to communication.

b. Information Overload: This is also a physical barrier as too much information can ruin communication completely. Communication should be in ample amounts but not excessive.

Psychological Barriers

a. Premature evaluation: This means preconceived notions, judgements, or opinions. This is a very common psychological barrier and must be kept at bay in any professional communication. Forming opinions before receiving the complete message can lead to miscommunication.

b. Emotions: These barriers arise from various intense emotions, which can distort understanding and hinder the expression of thoughts and feelings. Feelings such as anger, fear, anxiety, shame, jealousy, sadness etc are some emotions which can impede communication. If a receiver is going through any or most of these feelings then there are high chances of miscommunication. Therefore, this too is a barrier to communication. Extreme emotions hinder the effectiveness of communication.

c. Lack of background knowledge and interest: If the receiver has less or no knowledge on any topic then it can lead to miscommunication. Also, interest is essential for effective communication anywhere. You cannot communicate without interest and neither can you communicate to someone who is not interested in communicating. The subject matter needs to be of interest to both the sender as well as the receiver. Therefore, this too can act as a barrier to communication.

Cultural Barriers

a. Stereotyping: It is the most common cultural barrier to communication. This creates prejudices and impedes communication. In any professional setting stereotyping can be very detrimental to the company or firm and must not be practiced at all.

b. Ethnocentrism: Ethnocentrism as the name suggests is related to ethnic groups. It often results in viewing the world through the lens of one's own cultural norms and values, which can foster prejudice and division among groups. So, when one group considers themselves superior to another on pretext of ethnicity or race or colour or religion or class, then it is an example of ethnocentrism. This is again a very important and common barrier to communication which must be avoided.

So, these cultural barriers can significantly impact professional lives. It can lead to misunderstandings and misinterpretations among team members from different cultural backgrounds. All this leads to a reduced collaboration and sharing of diverse ideas. This can also disrupt overall workplace harmony. So, there is a need to ensure that all barriers to communication are addressed.

How to Overcome Barriers to Communication?

One of the most basic methods to overcome the barriers to communication as described above were given by Scott M. Cutlip and Allen H. Center who introduced the 7 Cs of communication in their 1952 textbook, *Effective Public Relations.*

7 Cs of Communication:

1. **Completeness**: The message to be sent must be complete in all respects. It should have all information that needs to be conveyed to the receiver. In professional communication there is a growing tendency to send messages in a hurry, thereby missing out on important information. This needs to be avoided. Message should be complete with all details and information and facts.

2. **Conciseness**: Message need not be too lengthy or too short as it will eventually beat the purpose of communication. Therefore, there is a need to be concise with the message as brevity is important in any communication. Hence, the message should be concise.

3. **Clarity**: If the message is not clear, then the purpose of communication is simply defeated. Message should be easy to understand and must be clear. Also, the sender must be clear about the purpose of the message.

4. **Concreteness**: The message should be concrete, i.e. must be definite, solid and vivid. Concrete words, images, phrases must be used to lead to effective communication.

5. **Correctness**: This means that the message must be grammatically and factually correct. One must ensure grammatical and syntactical correctness, and no spelling mistakes. Also, facts stated in any message must be correct.

6. **Consideration**: It means to be considerate of the audience. The receiver must be kept in mind always. The message should be considerate and must take into account the social background, past experience, expectations and mood of the receiver. You must consider the audience while communicating.

7. **Courtesy**: It means good, polite and acceptable behaviour of communication. It can also mean graceful politeness and decent behaviour. Courtesy is extremely important while communicating with your peers, seniors or juniors in any professional setting.

Therefore, we discussed the various barriers to communication and also the different ways in which communication can be made effective. Professional setting can easily lead to conflicts and moments of distress if communication is not up to the mark. The 7Cs technique must be kept in mind and must be made a part and parcel of our communication techniques to avoid any such mishap and to ensure proper and useful communication.

> "To effectively communicate, we must realize that we are all different in the way we perceive the world and use this understanding as a guide to our communication with others."
> -Tony Robbins

Activity/ Example

Look at this speech "Ain't* I a Woman?" delivered by Sojourner Truth (1797-1883)

[Sojourner Truth, American abolitionist (born Isabella Baumfree 1797-1883) was born into slavery in upstate New York. "Ain't I a Woman?" is her most famous speech, delivered in 1851 at the Women's Rights Convention in Akron, Ohio.]

Several ministers* attended the second day of the Woman's Rights Convention and were not shy in voicing their opinion of man's superiority over women. One claimed 'superior intellect', one spoke of the 'manhood of Christ', and still another referred to the 'sin of our first mother.'*

Suddenly, Sojourner Truth rose from her seat in the corner of the church. Sojourner walked to the podium and slowly took off her sunbonnet. Her six-foot frame towered over the audience. She began to speak in her deep resonant voice: …'That man over there says that women need to be helped into carriages and lifted over ditches and to have the best place everywhere. Nobody ever helps me into carriages or over mud-puddles or gives me any best place! And ain't I a woman?'

Sojourner raised herself to her full height. 'Look at me! Look at my arm.' She bared her right arm and flexed her powerful muscles. 'I have plowed, I have planted, and I have gathered into barns. And no man could head me. And ain't I a woman?' I could work as much and eat as much as man – when I could get it – and bear the lash as well! And ain't I a woman? I have borne children and seen most of them sold into slavery, and when I cried out with a mother's grief, none but Jesus heard me. And ain't I a woman?' The women in the audience began to cheer wildly.

'She pointed to another minister. 'He talks about this thing in the head. What's that they call it?'

'Intellect', whispered a woman nearby.

'That's it honey. What's intellect got to do with women's rights or black folks' rights?

'That little man in black there! He says women can't have as much rights as men, 'cause Christ wasn't a woman.' She stood with outstretched arms and eyes of fire. 'Where did your Christ come from? Where did your Christ come from?' she thundered again. 'From God and a Woman! Man had nothing to do with him!' The entire church now roared with deafening applause.

'If the first woman God ever made was strong enough to turn the world upside down all alone, these women together ought to be able to turn it back and get it right-side up again. And now that they are asking to do it the men better let them. I am obliged to you for hearing me, and now old Sojourner ain't got nothing more to say.'

*Ain't – Short form for "am I not"
*Minister – In the USA a minister is a priest in a church.

**Sin of our first Mother — reference to Eve eating the forbidden fruit and tempting Adam to eat it.*

Question

1. Find examples of **non-verbal communication** in this passage.

Non-verbal communication is all about expressing thoughts and feelings without the use of words. It harnesses the power of body language, facial expressions, gestures, posture, and eye contact. This form of communication is vital for revealing our emotions and intentions, often adding depth to our words. Some of the examples of non-verbal communication in this passage are:

• When the entire church roars with deafening applause, it shows that Truth has succeeded in the art of non-verbal communication as along with her speech her presence was super strong.

• Sojourner walking to the podium and slowly taking off her sunbonnet also shows her strong non-verbal communication. It shows she is in charge of the situation and comes across as a strong woman of substance.

• The Church roaring with deafening applause is also an example of non-verbal communication.

• When Sojourner Truth stood with outstretched arms it is an example of non-verbal communication. When Truth replied to the little man with fire in her eyes, it is also an example of non-verbal communication. Both these things show her strong persona and her strong image. This is also a part of non-verbal communication.

Question

2. What is feedback? Where do we find **feedback** to the speech in this passage?

Feedback is a reaction or a response from the receiver of the message to the sender. It confirms the receipt of the message and completes the communication cycle. These sentences show Feedback:

- "The women in the audience began to cheer wildly."
- "'Intellect', whispered a woman nearby."
- "The entire church now roared with deafening applause."

In the given passage, feedback can be found when the women in the audience begin to cheer wildly for Sojourner. It shows the woman is responding to the electric speech given by Sojourner.

When Sojourner Truth points at another minister and says, "He talks about this thing in the head. What's that they call it?" then a nearby women whispers, "Intellect". So, when the woman replies with "Intellect" to Sojourner's question, it shows that she is responding to the question posed by Sojourner. This is also feedback. Lastly, when the entire church applauds Sojourner's speech, it shows that the crowd loved her speech and respond with applause. It is also feedback. In these examples the feedback was the cheer, the reply, and the applause.

Question

3. Noise is defined as barrier that is generated within a message, and is caused by limited vocabulary, cultural differences, and blocked categories. Sojourner Truth is pointing to the male ministers in the room and refuting their points. What are the **possible barriers to communication** between Sojourner Truth and the male ministers?

Some of the barriers to communication in this case are:

- Psychological barrier, namely, distrust: The male ministers considered men superior over women and thus did not trust the words of Sojourner, a women's rights activist. Another psychological barrier is the premature evaluation. In the given speech, the male ministers made their opinion before receiving the message from the women. This premature evaluation prevents effective communication.
- Cultural barrier, namely, ethnocentrism: Sojourner was born into slavery and thus had led a very different life than the white male

ministers. This is example of ethnocentrism and is a huge cultural barrier between the two communities. This can lead to miscommunication. This is therefore a cultural barrier to communication. Another cultural barrier is the gender stereotype, which can be seen in the thoughts of the ministers who believe that Sojourner Truth is not equal to men.

Question

4. The **7 Cs** of effective communication are Completeness, Conciseness, Consideration, Clarity, Concreteness, Courtesy, and Correctness. Find examples of a few of these from the above speech.

- Conciseness: Sojourner's speech was not very long and yet she was able to convey her message clearly. The speech was short, precise and concise. She did not delve into unnecessary ramblings and was concise in her communication skills, therefore, making her speech highly effective. She spoke to the point and excelled in that.
- Clarity: Sojourner had a clear and strong voice and she was able to get her message across to the audience. Sojourner Truth kept her speech to the point and gave her message clearly that women are not inferior to men. This shows clarity of her thought and clarity of her expression. Lines like "If the first woman God ever made was strong enough to turn the world upside down all alone, these women together ought to be able to turn it back and get it right-side up again", communicates the idea in a clear manner. This is the importance of clarity in communication.
- Concreteness: Sojourner spoke strongly and painted a clear picture of her life and why the male ministers were wrong in their ideas of male superiority. Her arguments were concrete and therefore irrefutable and therefore she emerged as a strong orator and speaker. This is because she was concrete in her expression.
- Courtesy: Courtesy means graceful politeness and controlled language. Not once in her speech she used abusive language despite the provoking words of the male ministers. Truth ends her speech with polite courtesy and at the end said, "Obliged to you for hearing me." Therefore, her speech, though impassioned

and angry had courtesy which the male ministers in the audience did not have. So, courtesy is also a very important element in any communication. 'Obliged to you for hearing me, and now old Sojourner ain't got nothing more to say' is an example of courtesy.

• Correctness: Correctness denotes correct language, grammar, accurate facts and figures. Sojourner Truth made sure that she took the exact terms used by the ministers like, 'intellect', 'manhood of Christ', etc. Sojourner Truth stated her points clearly in front of ministers by using a real biological point like the birth of Christ. She said that Christ too came from a woman and not from a man. There is accuracy of facts and ideas in this. Therefore, the importance of correctness in any speech is extremely crucial as it lends validity to the statement.

So, through these various instances we understand the importance of the 7Cs of communication. In all areas of professional life, these 7Cs must be adhered to correctly.

Summary

In this unit we learned the basic concepts of communication as a subject. In order to master any skill, it is important to understand it well to its core so that learning and improving may become easy. Communication as a skill demands conceptual clarity and fundamental understanding from its learners. This unit discussed the basic concept of communication, what it means, and the significant role it plays in professional life. To understand the nuances of communication the beginning point is to understand its process. In this unit we learned about the Process of Communication which is also called Cycle of Communication because of its circular structure. The process of communication includes some major components which are crucial for successful communication. Lack or error in any of these components can make your communication poor and in worst cases the communication may even fail. These components include- sender, encoding, message, medium, channel, receiver, decoding, and feedback. These components are essential for a message to get transmitted successfully. The next important step of the communication process is feedback which this unit covers thoroughly. Feedback is the response or reply of the receiver whom the sender sends a message. Feedback is the process which completes the cycle of communication. This unit taught us the significance of feedback in professional life. It works as an assurance that the receiver has understood your message and it helps in clarifying any doubts or confusion, and most importantly it brings the response of the receiver to our message.

Communication as a subject and concept has been theorized by multiple theories. These scholars developed various models of communication which basically worked to help us understand the process of communication in a technical manner and gain insights into the working mechanism of communication. This unit explains the major theories and models of communication in an easy and simplified way for the students with a thorough conceptual clarity. These theories are significant to understand the development of communication as a subject over a period of time and its historical understanding in academia.

Communication is divided into various types based on its medium and we can use it as per our requirements. It is primarily divided into two parts – verbal and non-verbal. This unit discussed the difference between the two and their uses along with various examples. It also taught us about written communication which is mostly used in formal communication and is a major medium of professional correspondence.

One of the most important factors to ensure successful communication is the absence of communication barriers. Communication barriers are multiple types of obstacles that disturb the communication process and do not let the message get transmitted properly. The unit taught us about multiple types of communication barriers and ways to overcome them and ensure successful communication and avoid confusion. The 7Cs of communication form a range of ways through which the communication barriers can be avoided and dealt with. In this unit we learned how to use these 7 Cs and ensure complete, concise and clear communication.

Glossary

Barrier: Any type of obstacles, difficulties, or interruption in completion of a task or process is known as barriers.

Brevity: Something which has the quality of being brief or short.

Conciseness: The quality of explaining something completely and clearly in limited words.

Correspondence: Sending and receiving information. This term is mostly used for communication through writing letters.

Decode: Making or finding meaning out of a code or message. Understanding and making interpretation of a message.

Encode: To turn an information into a message.

Ethnocentrism: This is a belief that one's own culture or country is the best and superior to others. It views others as inferior and their own as the only parameter to judge others.

Globalization: Paced up intermingling of cultures, communities, and nations across the world. This term is commonly used in economic context.

Noise: A form of disturbance due to unwanted sounds. It is a barrier in communication.

Receiver: Someone who receives a message or the one whom a message is sent to by a sender.

Sender: Someone who sends a message.

Stereotype: A rigid belief, opinion or image about a particular community or group which is often incorrect. It is based on generalization and age-old prejudice and biases.

Transmitting: The act of sending or sharing something to a receiver.

Self-Assessment Questions

1. What is the role of noise in communication and how can cultural difference create breakdown of channels of communication?

2. Take any one social media flatform of your choice and exemplify how gatekeeping happens on such a platform.

3. How does racial prejudice shape communication prejudice?

4. What is ethnocentrisms in communication. Define with examples from any known culture.

5. Define the communication process with references to any three theoretical models of communication.

6. What is a sign within communication system?

References

Raman, Meenakshi, and Sharma, Sangeeta. *Technical Communication: Principles and Practice.* India, Oxford University Press, 2015.

Suggested Readings

Bhardwaj, Kumkum. *Professional Communication.* India, I.K. International Publishing House Pvt. Limited, 2013.

Quintanilla Miller, Kelly, and Wahl, Shawn T. *Business and Professional Communication: Keys for Workplace Excellence.* United States, SAGE Publications, 2019.

Tyagi, Kavita, and Misra, Padma. *Professional Communication.* India: philearning, 2010.

Unit 2
Professional Digital Communication in Social Space

Learning Objectives

This unit focuses on digital communication in the professional sphere. Digital communication stands for all types of transmission of information by using a digital mode. There are various sorts of digital modes which are used for communication, like text messages, phone calls, social media apps and online video calls. In the professional sphere digitalization has come as a boon. It saves time, energy and money to arrange an online meeting instead of a face-to-face meeting in the office. Nowadays multiple types of digital modes are used for teaching learning purposes as well. This unit brings you an in depth understanding of using social media and various digital platforms to utilize this technology for your benefit. The unit includes use of social media and how to use it for professional endeavours. Nowadays the internet has given us multiple sources to earn income, this unit teaches you various techniques along with a step-by-step guide to ace the skills of earning as a blogger and book reviewer. You will also learn the most in demand skill of creating your own CV and Resume with the help of tips and techniques along with multiple examples, catering a various range of job profiles which will help you build your own CV by the end of this book.

This unit includes skills to master in order to use the internet for the learning process as well. These skills include honing your note taking skills and audio listening skills which one can use to get the most of an online learning environment from the comfort of their home. The unit lastly but most importantly focuses on the importance of netiquettes while using social media and digital platforms in order to keep yourself and your data safe.

Introduction

Nowadays the internet has taken over our lives and we cannot imagine a day without using it. In the professional sphere, the internet plays a vital role in sustaining formal communication as well as in building a company's rapport with its customers and clients. This section will explain and demonstrate the various digital writing skills used in an organisation. These skills are very crucial in maintaining a professional outlook and will be beneficial in advancing your career. The book aims to develop writing techniques that can aid a student in their professional lives. The objective of this subsection is to provide some practical hands-on-skills through examples to explain the importance of digital communications in a fast-changing professional setting. Also, it is expected that students can gain first-hand experience of the requirements of the job market to prepare for it in advance.

We already know by now the rising significance of professional communications in a world where the private business sector will proliferate and along with it will also open large avenues for various career choices. We also know that the future of workforce in India is secured with the corporate sector which demands efficient professionalism and adroit communication skills. To prepare themselves for this dynamic sector, students need to learn the technical know-how of professional communications. These professional communication skills will enhance their candidature and increase their chances of securing a bright future within professional spaces. These communication skills will not only help the young job aspirants to secure but also to excel in their professional spaces with dynamism.

The forms of professional communications like social media posts (e.g. Twitter posts), blog writing, book-review writing, documentation, advertisements, invitations, poster designing on Canva, LinkedIn profiles, CV/ Resume writing, etc. can be categorised as core digital professional communications. This is because they rely solely on our knowledge and competence in using digital platforms to create them. These forms of digital communications are very important in any business organisation. We will be learning the art of proper documentation for a business organisation. The professional candidature of a candidate relies on the strength of a candidate's CV. Hence, we will be learning the art of creating useful CVs/ resume, job-application letters, and the usage of professional handles like LinkedIn. The students will also be introduced to Canva and its importance in digital communications.

This topic will allow the readers to a more seasoned approach towards some major social media platforms like Twitter & Facebook. Nowadays, many organisations and companies monitor your social media handle to assess your job candidature. It is therefore essential that we all maintain social media etiquettes in a responsible manner.

The topic is not about how to use Facebook or Twitter. Here the discussion is more focussed on how to engage audience and how to appear presentable on social media platforms. This is essential in this highly connected world where social media presence matters a lot in any business setting. Digital Communication is the buzzword in this age. Digital communication is important not just at the individual but also at the professional level. The rise of internet has given wide range of opportunities to engage in digital communication which was inconceivable some decades ago. However, there is still a need to understand some basics of digital communications w.r.t. some major digital platforms like Facebook and Twitter.

Focus would be given more on how to use digital communication in businesses. In a world which is getting increasingly connected online the importance of digital marketing cannot be underestimated. More and more people nowadays, of all age groups, are using internet for their day to day lives. And in the coming days this is bound to increase. It has been seen that many organisations now ask for the social media details of the candidates who apply for jobs. This is because social media responsibility has now become a keyword for many organisations. Hence, under such a scenario it is all the more vital that we learn and ingrain social media skills to communicate ourselves better on a social channel like Twitter, Facebook, etc.

Social media etiquettes are not just about personal communication but it is equally important for business communication as well. This is the reason why any business, firm or organisation nowadays create their own Facebook and Twitter handle. It is necessary to create an impact in the business world and these social media platforms give them a stage to do so.

> "The Internet has changed everything. We expect to know everything instantly. If you don't understand digital communication, you're at a disadvantage."
> -Bob Parsons

How to Write on Social Media?

1. Assess which social media platform works best for you. Social media may be free but it consumes time and energy. Hence, there is a need to understand which works best for you.

2. The old-style social communication methods will eventually turn obsolete. Now is the time to turn digital.

3. One must find their own social media voice and should be emotive while expressing on social media. The use of emojis is equally important.

4. Do not get too involved in social media. As already mentioned, social media is free but it takes up your time. Excess exposure to social media can be dangerous and detrimental to one's health.

5. Social media is a great tool for each and every one of us to have and present our own independent view point. Hence, social media should be seen as an enabler in a democratic set up as it gives an open forum to all.

6. While writing a social media post, it can be observed that asking a question at the end of the post leads to increased engagement of audience.

7. A social media post should never be a long, drab textual material. It should always be complemented with visuals. Images,

videos, GIFs & emojis play a very important role in communicating in a digital space. But take due care not to overdo it.

8.   Nowadays you can connect all of your social media channels through one link. There is a provision to attach your Instagram, LinkedIn profile, Twitter handle within one single social media platform.

9.   Always try to use catchy captions while posting on social media. Social media is all about expressing in a unique manner. Carefully curated captions can be a great eye catcher to your profile.

10. Use idioms, phrases and popular proverbs in your social media posts. It lends accuracy and liveliness to your post.

11. On your social media profile, make sure you fill all details about your bio.

12. Use hashtags effectively on your posts. Hashtags are a great way to express some buzzword or emotion in a post.

13. You can create events through Facebook and be up to date with latest events, webinars and other functions.

> "The good thing about social media is it gives everyone a voice. The bad thing is ... it gives everyone a voice."
> -Brian Solis

Twitter

Twitter is arguably the only platform which has the widest reach among all its peers like Facebook, Instagram, LinkedIn, Pinterest, etc. Particularly for businesses, Twitter is an essential platform as it has the ability to connect on a much larger scale. It can be used to manage customer services and interaction with customers, to promote a company, to create important engagements and to share news and stay updated.

How to Engage Audience on Twitter?

Let us understand some ways in which we can engage our audience on Twitter. Some of the ways are –

- Use strong opening lines. The first few words should grab attention, as users scroll quickly. Start strong. The first few words should capture attention of the viewers.

- Twitter usernames should be simple so that your friends can find you easily. Username should be short and memorable.

- Clear and compelling 'Bio' makes your presence felt before even engaging with your profile. Make sure your bio clearly states who you are and what you do, including relevant keywords. This helps users understand your value and encourages them to follow you. Twitter Bio should contain professional details about you, like your job profile and designation.

- Twitter usernames must sound professional in nature as you can attach your Twitter profile URL to your CV/ Resume etc. while applying for jobs. Don't use a spammy username.

- Twitter is a crucial public as well as professional space where you can connect to your customers easily.

- Always use hashtags on Twitter. Twitter is a great platform to create narratives. Using hashtags makes it easy to do so. Engage with trending hashtags and if applicable, participate in trending hashtags to broaden your tweet's reach.

- Using hashtags catches people's attention. It also shows that you have given thought to your content by suffixing adequate hashtags.

- Check Twitter analytics to analyse which tweets perform best to understand what resonates with your audience.

- Be Mindful of your tone always. Tone can be easily misinterpreted in text, so ensure your message is clear and respectful.

- The art of tweeting can be said to be the art of tweeting in 280-characters only. It is meant to convey something in a much shorter way. Tweets should be short and concise. With Twitter's character limit, every word counts. Make your message clear and compelling from the start to capture attention.

- A good Tweet will make your viewer stop and read your post instead of scrolling over it.

- Also, lengthy texts and posts are mostly overwhelming and tedious to read. Short sentences make text readable.

- Engagement with the followers is most important in Twitter. Always reply to comments as it shows that you are active and engaged by responding to comments and mentions.

- Retweet and Like posts. Support others by retweeting and liking their content, which can help build relationships and connections too. It is an underrated technique to increase Twitter engagement. Show your engagement by replying to comments and mentions.

- During any social media post, always be conversational rather than controversial. It opens up new possibilities and creates a more humane and beneficial social media outreach.

- Interact regularly with your audience. Replying to comments, retweeting interesting content, and engaging in conversations go a long way. This not only builds relationships but also increases your visibility on the platform.

- Use humour and relatability. Humour can make your tweets more shareable, as long as it aligns with your brand or the idea that you are propounding in the tweet.

Practice
How can you use social media to connect with people and businesses?

"With Twitter and other social networking tools, you can get a lot of advice from great people. I learn more from Twitter than any survey or discussion with a big company."
-Daniel Ek

Book Review Writing

A Book Review is usually a short form of literary review or literary criticism which analyses a book based on various parameters such as style, content and relevance.

Nowadays, book reviews are professional paid jobs and require much technical skills. Book reviews can be of opinion types or summary types as well. It tries to summarise the entire book by highlighting the key areas of the book. It also gives the opinion of a reviewer and shows how they think about the book.

How to write a Book Review?

1.   A book review has no stipulated length. It can be of any length but should be complete in itself. However, certain websites ask for a particular length so you must adhere to the word limit.

2.   A Review must have a heading or title. Try to give a creative heading. One way to write a good heading is to focus on keywords in the book.

3.   Take special care not to give away the name of the major characters. Do not spoil the plot for other readers. Do not reveal the ending. You have to learn how to just provide the brief overview without giving up crucial details. Summarize the book's main themes, plot, or arguments, but avoid giving away major spoilers. Focus on the key elements that define the book, such as its genre, setting, or central conflict.

4.   A reviewer must mention their favourite parts in a review. This will give some additional perspective to the readers. Share your personal thoughts on the book. What aspects did you enjoy, and what did not resonate with you? Be detailed in discussing things like the writing style, character development, pacing, or structure.

5.   Give special attention to grammatical errors in the original book which you are reviewing. Formatting and spacing must be given special attention. If there are errors of this sort then it must be mentioned in the final review.

6.   A book review should be general in tone and opinion. Was it interesting to read, or good, or tiresome, or slow or bad?

7.   While writing a book review, you should decide if you are going to write a favourable review in favour of the author or you are warning other readers not to purchase the book.

8.   Give special mention to the key highlights of the book. If there is anything which strikes you as a reader, mention it in the review.

9. It is always better not to summarise the book in a review. A review is not about what has happened in the book. It should be more about what to expect in the book.

10. Quote a few lines from the original book. A small passage or two is also acceptable. This will give your readers an example of what to expect from the book.

11. Give special mention to any character(s) that stand out. Also write about the plot construction.

12. Assess the book's position in its genre. Compare the book to others in the same genre or by the same author. Consider its originality, relevance, and how it contributes to the genre to which it belongs.

13. In a book review, you may also give grades, ratings, or stars to be more objective, clear and fair about your review. You can give star rating too. Like ★★, ★★★, ★★★★, ★★★★★ to show the level of recommendation to your audience.

Example of a Book Review of *The Shadow Lines* (1988) by Amitav Ghosh

<u>Book Review</u>

The Shadow Lines (1988)
Author: Amitav Ghosh

The Shadow Lines is a historical fiction novel which got Amitav Ghosh the Sahitya Akademi award in 1990. Published in 1988, the novel is set in Calcutta during the period of India-Bangladesh partition and the communal riots that broke at that time.

The story revolves around the unnamed narrator whose life is heavily influenced by his intellectual and eccentric uncle Tridib to the extent that the narrator emerges as the alter ego of Tridib. Tridib can be seen as the protagonist of the novel. He is a young man who is usually found in his room drowned in a book with a cigarette in his hand or gossiping with passersby at the Gole Park. He meets a tragic end that captures the pain of the riots realistically. The story begins with the narrator reminiscing about his childhood days in Calcutta when he was 8 years old. The novel is a bildungsroman that depicts the growth of the narrator from an eight-year-old child till he is a fully grown adult. The novel can be seen as being psychological in nature as well because it focuses a lot on the narrator's inner thoughts and struggles. He lives in the memory of the past. Memory plays an important part in the novel. It is only because of his memory of Tridib that the narrator has treasured throughout his life that has made him travel the places he has never been to.

The title of the novel *The Shadow Lines* symbolizes the borders between the nations that are made with bloodshed which are arbitrary like the shadow lines. The writing style of the novel is in the first-person narration. The narration of the novel is rather complex as there are multiple stories being told by multiple characters and the timeline keeps shifting but this is where the beauty of Ghosh's narrative style lies. The style is inimitable and a unique narrative voice makes the novel stand out in flesh and blood in front of the readers.

All the stories told by multiple characters are filtered in the voice of the unnamed narrator. The major themes of the novel are history, time, partition, imagination, freedom, and memory. The novel also shows relationship dynamics between multiple characters and how they change. The novel explores how personal relationships are affected by the political turmoil. The other major characters of the novel are Thamma, the narrator's grandmother; Ila, the narrator's cousin whom he secretly loves and May, Tridib's girlfriend who later reveals the "final redemptive mystery" to the narrator, a revelation of a painful memory that May always carried with her which brings to the narrator the truth behind Tridib's death. The characters are convincingly drawn and each character is created with a sense of realism.

The novel is hailed as a literary masterpiece and rightly so. Reading it is an experience of its kind. This novel is highly recommended to everyone who wants to read about the experiences of partition and how it affected people personally and politically. Besides providing historical insights the novel is highly recommended for its brilliant storytelling and rich literariness.

Rating ★★★★★ (**5 Star Rating**); Highly Recommended.
 # Reviewer's choice

> "I mean, when you're tired of book reviews, you're tired of life."
> -Lev Grossman

Blog Writing

A 'Blog' is a kind of a weblog, or an online repository where you can share your thoughts, ideas, discussions in an open sphere. It is like a personal log, where you may share personalised stuff. Blogging is a social and networking tool to connect with new people. It is a great way to connect with like-minded people. Nowadays blogging has become very popular. It is accessible to all and anyone can create their own blog. Blogging is universal and free for all.

A blog is created with an intention to spread your ideas to the wider audience. It is like a personal website but is free for the creator.

A blog is a very versatile space. It can be used for various purposes. A blog can be a great place to share personal thoughts, discuss on some crucial pressing issues. It can be used to fulfil one's creative purposes and needs. A blog can be a place where you may also publish book reviews, essays, commentary on movies and hold discussions for your visitors. Basically, everything under the sun can be discussed and can find a place in a blog.

Blogging is also a great way to a career in successful marketing and social networking.

Blogging is basically communicating your area of interest and generating fruitful discussions on it.

Some major domain names which can be used for creating your own individual blogs -

- https://www.livejournal.com/
- https://www.blogger.com/about/
- https://wordpress.com/

Among these the most popular and widespread is wordpress.com. You will find most of the blogs are associated with wordpress.com. This is because it is free and allows you customisation and you can personalise your own blog freely as per your own preferences.

Tips for Blog Writing:

- You must always consider your readers while writing a blog.
- Readers are known as visitors and they will be your primary audience. So, you must understand the taste of your visitors.
- You can always start a general blog about general topics where you may invite your friends and family members to visit.
- Always follow some famous and major blogs to learn new ideas, contribute to discussions and to get engaging ideas.
- Blog is like an ongoing discussion and continuous dialogues on certain topics. Hence, blogs should always be open ended. It must invite discussions rather than concluding it.
- Selection of blog topic is crucial in writing a blog. Take topics which are from your area of interest like cricket, cooking, politics, literature, make-up and cosmetics, stock markets, etc.
- Always take a topic which can keep you hooked on for many years. Make a list of topics and select one or two topics to write a blog on.
- Always keep a separate email list ready with you to send the blog to your friends and visitors. This will help you recognise target audience and make them visit your blog too.
- Write in paragraphs as well as use pictures and graphic images to make it visually appealing. Illustrate your topic with images.
- Use appropriate headlines and keywords to make your blog stand out.
- Create a Facebook or Instagram or Pinterest profile for your blog with the same name.
- Any blog can be successful only if it is regular and consistent. Chart out an event calendar for your blog where you

keep posting regularly in regular intervals.

- Always attach your blog with your other social media sites, like Twitter, Facebook, Instagram, Pinterest, etc. This will broaden your audience.

- Create an eye-catchy blog name. It should be short, simple and creative.

- Social media is a great enabler in our society today. But there is a dark side to it as well. Social media can be a great way to troll and demean others and can generate a toxic environment. It is better to stay clear from such controversies. Blogs should be a place to generate fruitful discourses and not negative discourses.

- You can use Google Analytics, a software to track your visitors. You need a Google account to use it. You must monitor the visitors who are coming to your blog.

- Add content regularly or your blog will become obsolete. Consistency is required to become an effective blogger.

> "If you want to continually grow your blog, you need to learn to blog on a consistent basis."
> -Neil Patel

Making Online Academic/ Work Profile – LinkedIn

LinkedIn is an online service that is employment-centred. It is an America based business service. It was founded in 2002. It is very useful for creating networks in professional areas and for career related developments. It is widely used by employers to post about jobs and by people who seek jobs to share their resume and CV.

It might not be wrong to call LinkedIn profile as your own online resume. A basic LinkedIn profile is free to all and hence every person who wishes to get into professional life should have a LinkedIn profile. Even college graduates should create their own profile.

Nowadays LinkedIn is a great platform for job applicants to get in touch with prospective employers for jobs. It is very essential for anyone entering the job field to create their own profile on LinkedIn which can also help them to land job offers easily.

Why use LinkedIn?

- It is the biggest platform in the world for creating networks professionally. It is an amazing platform for anyone searching for a job. It can help you find the type of job you are looking for.
- It is useful for strengthening professional relations and learning the important skills for your career growth.
- LinkedIn provides you with a personal brand of your own on an online platform and allows you to showcase your knowledge and ability here which attracts the right type of job opportunities for you.
- LinkedIn can be used as a great tool to research for upcoming interviews and career opportunities.
- LinkedIn allows people to recommend you that helps your employers know that your abilities are reliable and backs you for your abilities and skills.
- You can follow companies that you are interested in working with to learn more about them.
- The platform is widely used for professional groups. They help you in learning and gaining more experience from others and get to know more people and build professional relations.

> "Three years ago, we said you'd have to think long and hard about hiring a recruiter with less than a couple of hundred LinkedIn connections. Now the same holds true for candidates in general."
> **-Kris Dunn**

How to use LinkedIn?

1. You need a formal official picture for your LinkedIn profile to make it look official and business like in nature. Using a picture on LinkedIn profile is extremely significant.
2. Do not wear casual clothes or put casual pictures on your LinkedIn profile.

3.   Never put selfies on your LinkedIn profile.

4.   Your employment title, job information and professional career must be up to date in the profile.

5.   Always proofread whatever you add in your LinkedIn profile. There should be no room for errors as it will appear very unprofessional to your employer.

6.   Make a list of your skills which you possess for your online profile. These skills must be attuned to your work experience and interests. This goes a long way in ensuring your credibility towards your professional career and it creates a good impression on the interviewer.

7.   Always be willing to learn and view other professional profiles to see how you can improve your own profile.

8.   Follow LinkedIn profiles which are from your area of interest. Follow organisation and companies that you wish to work with. You will remain updated about the job alerts in that case.

Practice

Q1. What is the significance of LinkedIn in professional life?
Q2. Create your own professional LinkedIn profile.

Netiquettes

The word *netiquette* is made up of two words *net* and *etiquette*. The set of rules of conduct that we should follow while communicating respectfully and appropriately on the Internet is known as netiquettes. It is also known as the "etiquettes of the internet".

The netiquettes are not one of the legal rules that must be followed but they are recommended rules that should be followed as a part of etiquettes. The use of this term mostly revolves around communicating with strangers on the internet. Netiquettes include different types of rules that largely depend on the type of platform and its users. In most of the cases the app or the website have their own set of netiquettes which they explain to their users. It makes the applications and the websites responsible for keeping an eye on the sites to make sure that their netiquettes are being followed by their users. In case there occurs any violation of these rules, the apps and websites must take actions against the violator. But apart from that, netiquettes are a very basic yet important part of communication which everybody needs to learn and understand in order to get better at communication and learn to maintain an appropriate amount of basic decency.

Netiquettes - Significance in Professional Life

Today we are living in the age of the internet where the first thing our day begins with is checking our social media apps. Similarly, it ends with a scroll on social media. Social media occupies a large and significant place in our lives and it is an important part of our personal and professional life. Especially after the pandemic, the internet has taken over our lives. So as the use of the internet and its importance has been increasing, it is important for us to pay attention to using the internet appropriately and make it a safe space to connect, express and create. In professional life, social media plays a big role as the social media profile of a candidate or member of a company is often seen as an extension of their personality, and as a part of the company what they post can be seen as coming from the representatives of the company. Hence, the most important thing when it comes to netiquettes or using the internet with etiquettes is that we need to always keep in mind that whatever we post will be our responsibility and we should be mindful of it. It is important to understand that on social media we are talking to people, who are real, living human beings and not just an account on social media. We should behave on the internet the way we behave in real life, with decency and etiquettes. Just like the real world where etiquettes are important, we should follow netiquettes on the internet as well.

Netiquettes – Skills for Communication

Like any other skill that we learn through practice, it is possible to master netiquettes as well. Improving netiquette involves fostering a more respectful, constructive, and positive online environment. Here are some ways to enhance netiquette:

- One must always stick to the rules of communication that they would follow in their real life. It includes treating people with kindness and decency, the way we behave in real life, and keeping in mind that all of us are humans behind the screens.

- We need to also make sure that the words we use while composing a message should be proper and appropriate. Your message should not have any derogatory word and you should avoid using foul language.

- The internet is a place where people assume they can let their frustration out on anyone in the form of criticism. This should be avoided. Taking and receiving criticism are both difficult tasks, especially on the internet. But one needs to be careful with their choice of words while criticizing others. And it is important to make sure that one's criticism is constructive and is coming from a place of hope for the other person. It must come with an aim to do better and not from a personal dislike.

- One of the most important aspects of the internet is privacy. We need to make sure to not misuse anyone's personal information that was shared by them.

- Most of the content we see on social media and the internet is available for free. So, here it is our responsibility to give credits to the rightful owner of the content who holds all of the copyrights, while sharing it on our social media.

- Bullying has become very common on the internet. One should never indulge in bullying anyone over any matter. And if you find yourself or somebody else getting bullied on the internet, then you must take legal actions against it.

- Recording or saving others' data without their consent is wrong and can get you charged. When someone posts their pictures online or shares content during a presentation, their pictures and content is considered their own data which they have a copyright over. Reposting someone's content as your own is wrong and one should also never post it without their permission.

- While communicating on the internet there are many factors that come in our way to express ourselves properly. So it becomes even more important to express yourself on the internet and make sure your grammar and words are correct.

- The internet has provided us with multiple instant messaging apps that induce a sense of restlessness when people do not reply instantly. Although it is one of the most basic, yet important netiquettes to respond to your texts, messages, and emails on time, at the same time it is important to provide space as well and let people take their time to respond and get back to us.

- One should avoid indulging in hate speech and always remember to be kind with people, even with the strangers that we communicate with on the Internet.

- Increasing awareness about netiquette through education, especially in schools and among new internet users such efforts should be aimed to emphasize the importance of respectful communication and online behaviour.

- Demonstrating courteous and respectful behaviour in your own online interactions such that others may follow suit when they see positive examples.

- Encouraging users to consider the feelings and perspectives of others before posting or commenting it promotes empathy as a guiding principle in online interactions.

- Clear outline netiquette guidelines on platforms and forums. Ensure users understand expectations for behaviour, language use, and interactions. Enforcing netiquette guidelines consistently. Implement moderation policies that address violations promptly and fairly. This helps maintain a healthy online community.

- Encourage constructive feedback and discussions. Discourage flame wars, trolling, and other forms of negative or disruptive behaviour.

- Respect cultural differences and diverse viewpoints. Foster an inclusive environment where all voices are valued and heard.

- Avoid overusing caps lock, emojis, or excessive punctuation that can be perceived as shouting or aggressive. Use tools like spell check to ensure clear communication.

- Teach users to critically evaluate information and sources before sharing or reacting. Help them understand the impact of their words and actions online.

• Regularly gather feedback from users about netiquette practices. Use this input to refine guidelines and improve the online community experience.

By keeping these points in mind, we can always be mindful and indulge in socially and professionally acceptable social media behaviour. By actively promoting and practicing these principles, we can collectively contribute to a more positive and respectful online environment, where netiquette becomes ingrained in everyday online interactions.

> "It's good netiquette to empathize with others online. It builds strong internet relationships."
> **-David Chiles**
> *The Principles of Netiquette*
> NetworkEtiquette.net

Audio-Book Listening

What are Audio Books?

The records of using audio books in schools trace back to the 1960's. With the rise of technology, audio books' popularity has increased over time. A recorded version of a book being read out loud is known as an audio book. Audio books are a great tool to help children in learning how to read. It has been proven to make improvements in reading comprehension as well. It is important to note that the use of audiobooks is not limited to only cater to the needs of children but adults as well can benefit from it. The format of audio books makes them an effective tool in learning and improving one's listening practice. Audio books are helpful in making the process of learning and gaining knowledge more accessible to people who have visual impairment. The use of audio books can also make the learning process easy for people whose learning abilities are not conventional and to those who are easily distracted. This is because audiobooks demand attention to comprehend the content of it which eventually improves listening skills.

> "Long before writing, people were telling each other stories and the audiobook goes all the way back to that tradition"
> -Philip Pullman

Audio-Book Listening – Why is it important?

Many people have this misconception that audio-books only cater to the needs of children who have learning disabilities, people who are learning a second language and the people who struggle with reading or who are non-readers. Although, audio-books have been a great help in providing these students an access to enjoying literature and books, the usefulness of audio-books is not limited to it. Audio-books can be a useful tool for all readers, here are a few ways in which audio-books can be helpful:

1. The biggest plus point of audio-books is that they are portable. Audio-books can be heard at any time on your smartphone. You can also access them through a smart speaker or a computer or laptop or a tablet like a Kindle reader.

2. Another thing that makes the audio-books more fun than the printed book is that you get to listen to the story. The storytelling by skilled and professional narrators makes the experience of learning the story and the plot much more interesting. It adds a dramatic effect too to the reading.

3. Listening to audio-books is not time consuming and it can be done at any time. It helps you include more reading in your busy daily routine as you can listen to audio-books even when you cannot read, for instance, while driving or cooking.

4. The greatest advantage of audio-books is that they allow you to multitask. You can listen to them at any time, when you are working out at the gym, while taking your pet on a walk, completing your household chores, gardening or while traveling.

5. You can listen to audio-books in the dark. As there are many places where you do not have electricity for example, while camping or simply when you do not want to disturb your roommate by turning the lights on, you can still listen to the audio-books and learn in the dark unlike printed books.

6. When it comes to learning a new language one of the most important things that determine your proficiency in it are your learning skills. Audio-books are a great help to learn a new language. It will improve your listening skills in the new language that you are learning.

7. Printed books come with their aesthetic hardcovers but there is a downside to it. Reading for long hours from hardcover books makes it difficult to hold it. But with audio books you can let go of this load!

8. You can include more people in it. audio books can be used in a group as many students can listen to it at one time. It is a great way for teachers to divide students into small groups and make them listen to the audio book and initiate and get involved in discussions with their peers. It not only helps in improving listening skills but it also plays an important role in encouraging critical thinking and practicing critical listening skills in students as well as improving focus.

> "Books are made out of paper. Paper is made out of trees."
>
> "Audiobooks?"
>
> "Audiobooks speak for themselves."
>
> **-Paul Acampora**
> *I Kill the Mockingbird*

Note-Taking

Note taking is an important technique that is helpful in effectively collecting information from multiple sources. It is particularly helpful in retaining the information on what somebody has just said or it may be useful during a lecture too. Students can make their learning process more effective with the help of note taking that is essential in order to retain and revisit the lessons learned at the time of examination. Note taking is an important part of the learning process, be it taking notes from a lecture, book, recording or any media or online material and it is important for students to master the technique of note taking in order to make their learning process most effective. To succeed in one's academic career, it is extremely important for a student to be able to take notes clearly and comprehensively. Effective note taking is useful for students in understanding and learning the material of their course in order to perform well in their assignments and exams. Good note taking is also useful to get back to one's old notes and it can be a great source to rely on during examinations.

Relevance in Professional Life

Note taking is a skill that is useful in all aspects of life and especially in professional life. Its usefulness is not limited to the academic sphere but it is an important skill at your workplace as well and using it effectively can be beneficial in your day-to-day professional life.

There are many ways through which note taking can be useful, some of which are:

1. Note taking is helpful in order to make you pay attention as it demands you to be attentive to the speaker or the source of information. It helps in improving your focus because now there is a certain thing to pay attention to. It is also helpful in remembering the ideas that you note down.

2. You will be able to recognize more easily what is significant and what is not.

3. Through note taking you can have permanent access to the material that you have learned from a lecture or a chapter which you have read, in the form of your notes.

4. When you have your notes, you can review them on a regular basis. It will help you in remembering the important stuff that somebody has told you or something that you have read. The practice of note taking is also helpful in organizing your thoughts and ideas.

5. When you take notes during a lecture, you actively look for the important things that need to be taken down. This allows your brain to be fully present during the lecture and it is helpful in

understanding the lecture properly by which you are able to filter out important information, which includes important facts, quotes, data and terms.

6. Note taking is particularly helpful when you have to note down information in a hurry or when the speaker is speaking at a fast pace. For example, during a lecture you might not have the time to write down each and every word your professor is speaking. In this situation you would only note down the important information by using abbreviations, symbols and just short points. This is why note taking plays a significant role in retaining the important information.

Another example:

Imagine when you are alone at your place and you receive a phone call. It is from your colleague, Neelam. She has some important information to share with you. You ask her to wait for a minute while you find a pen and notepad to note down the message. Look at what Neelam says regarding the last minute change of meeting:

Neelam: *Hello! Had to inform you that today's timing for the meeting with the Head Manager has been changed. Instead of 5:30 PM, it would be at 6:00 PM. Apologies for the inconvenience but the delay was unavoidable. Please inform all your team members to cooperate and join the meeting link sent to them all. Thank you. See you at 6:00 PM.*

If you knew the skills of note taking, it might have been written like this by you:

Neelam: meet time chngd frm @ 5:30 to @ 6:00. Inform team, join link.

So, you would not have to note down each and every word that the speaker, Neelam had spoken on the call. Instead, you would only note down major facts related to the event in discussion, namely, change of time. This major fact is the most important thing that needs to be remembered by your memory. This practice is what we call note-taking.

> "Research reveals the main value of note-taking is through its effect on how you encode the information in your brain. That is, the act of note-taking is more important than the result."
> **-Fiona McPherson**
> *Effective Notemaking*

How to Take Notes Effectively?

It is common among many people to face trouble when they go through their notes in understanding what they had earlier noted down. You can get rid of this struggle if you understand the right way to take notes. The most important thing while taking notes is paying attention. When you are attending a lecture, you should make sure that you're being attentive and focused and then you should listen carefully, think and write.

Here are some tips for taking notes effectively:

1. If you make handwritten notes, make sure you have enough paper to write on. Instead of using small pieces of paper, you should have full size sheets of paper to write on.

2. Make sure you have properly functional pens/ pencils.

3. You should start every new chapter or lecture on a new sheet or a new document in case you take notes digitally on phone or laptop. This will help you in organizing your notes and avoid confusion.

4. Articles like a, an, the, should not be used in making notes. They are not important when you are taking notes.

5. It is important for you to make sure that your writing is clearly readable so you do not face trouble reading your notes later.

6. If you are reading from a passage, you can still underline (___) or encircle important points or place an asterisk/ star (*) in its place. Doing this will ensure that you make notes effectively within the long-written text.

7. Using abbreviations and symbols are important and useful while taking notes. But make sure you understand the abbreviations and symbols well and avoid creating new abbreviations. Symbols such as: & for (and), + for (add, plus), − for (less, minus), ₹ for (rupees, money), % for (percent), @ for (at), ? for (question) can be used.

8. It is useful to write down the date and topic of the lecture or meeting you are taking notes of. It helps in keeping your notes well organized.

9. Notes of every subject should be kept together in your notebook or as files in your computer. It allows easy access to your notes.

10. Re-read your notes after the lecture or class. Re-reading will inculcate the habit of retaining. Notes must be revisited later on or else there is a high probability that you might forget your own notes.

11. Avoid skipping lines, unless the topic or idea that your teacher is speaking about is changed.

12. Leaving some space at the margins is another useful technique as it allows you to correct your notes and add your new ideas without creating a mess with your main notes.

13. Avoid wasting time by using an eraser instead just cut down the mistake you make while taking notes.

14. Some important things like a formula or a definition should be noted down word to word as heard by you.

15. It is an important part of note making to avoid writing down whole sentences. You should only write down major ideas, factual information and keywords.

16. There is no need to use articles while taking notes such as, a, an and the.

17. In order to highlight important words you can make circles, underline it and use asterisks (*) as well. You can also try using a highlighter pen to highlight important things.

18. It is very common to miss out on some information during a lecture. In such a situation you should not worry, instead just try leaving some space on your sheet so you can add the missed information later to your notes. You can ask your teacher or your classmate to share the part of the information you missed.

19. Make sure your mind is focused the most, on the central ideas of the topic you are learning and taking notes on during your lecture.

> "I never wrote things down to remember; I always wrote things down so I could forget."
> **-Matthew McConaughey**

Speedwriting Abbreviations:

I am here sharing a few words which can be used while making notes to write speedily. One of the best ways to make your own personalised abbreviation list is to remove the vowels (a, e, i, o, u) from the original word. Also, some words like difference, different, difficult might have similar abbreviations. In this case you must make out the meaning of the shortened phrase by looking at the larger context of the notes.

WORD	ABB	WORD	ABB	WORD	ABB
about	abt	after	aftr	adult	Adlt
according	acc	algebra	alg	american	Amer
activity	act	arrive	arriv	article	artcl
actually	actly	attention	attn	august	Aug
beautiful	btfl	because	bcoz/ becz	benefit	bnft
between	btw	biology	bio	brother	bro
camera	cam	capital	cap	character	char
college	colg	company	co.	continue	cont.
december	dec	develop	dev	discuss	dscuss
difference	diff	difficult	diff	different	diff
eastern	estrn	economic	eco	education	edu
election	elec	english	eng	environment	environ
everybody	evrbdy	everyone	evry1	everything	evrthng
family	fam	father	fathr	february	feb

finish	fin	forget	4get	friday	fri
geometry	geo	geology	geo	geography	geo
garden	grdn	great	gr8	government	govt
history	hist	hospital	hosptl	hundred	100
increase	inc	information	info	individual	indvdl
january	jan	july	jul	june	jun
knowledge	knwldg	keyboard	kybrd	kitchen	ktchn
language	lang	legal	legl	light	lite
magazine	mag/ magzn	monday	mon	march	mar
market	mkt	medical	med	medicine	med
necessary	nec	network	net	nothing	noth
number	#	november	nov	newspaper	nwspapr
october	oct	often	oft	ofcourse	ofc
people	ppl	phone no	ph no.	picture	pic
possibl	psbl	population	popul	problem	prob
quality	qual	quantity	qty	question	?
recognize	rec/ recog	responsible	resp	return	ret
saturday	sat	september	sept	second	2nd
section	sec	sunday	sun	size	sz
table	tbl	technology	tech	television	tv
thursday	thur	tuesday	tues	tonight	2night
understand	undrstnd	understood	undrstd	umbrella	umbrla

violence	vio	victim	vic	visual	vsl
wednesday	wed	webpage	wbpg	website	wbst
woman	wom	with respect to	wrt	work	wrk
x-rated	xratd	x-ray	xry	xerox	xrx
you	u	year	yr	yard	yd.
zigzag	zgzg	zebra	zbra	zee	z

Note: There are millions of words in the dictionary. You can make your own abbreviations on your own. The table above serves as a representative example only. You can modify some rules while making abbreviations. This is because in any professional setting your own notes need to be understood by you firstly. So, you can modify your own technique by mastering such words while taking down notes in a meeting.

E-Mail Writing

Email is one of the most commonly used mediums of communication in Professional sphere. The letter 'e' in email stands for 'electronic' which denotes it to be a digital method of communication. Unlike other digital mediums of communication like WhatsApp messages, Instagram DMs and other text and SMS, email is used for formal conversations. When you have to reach out to your professor to discuss an assignment you reach out to them through email to schedule an appointment. When you have to raise a query regarding the malfunction of a product you bought you have to raise your concern via email to the company. And when you have to apply for a job you are supposed to send your CV and job application through email to your recruiters. In our digitalized world emails play an important role in keeping the conversations going and connecting people and various organizations in building professional ties.

Significance in Professional Life

Communication in professional sphere cannot be imagined without the use of emails. Email has become the most easily accessible and convenient option for formal communication. From sending your CV and job application to applying for a job to scheduling meetings and sharing information with your clients email has made life easier for us. It plays a significant role as a digital medium of communication in saving time. It is more convenient than face to face conversations and much cheaper than phone calls. Email is an easy medium to share information quickly. Its various features such as scheduling mails, searching for an important mail through etc make it an easily accessible option. It also provides them with the freedom to respond as per our convenience unlike phone calls. Because of its various features that cater to the quick transmission of information and accessibility for multiple needs, emails are essential for professional communication.

Ways to Enhance E-mail Writing

Here are some suggestions to make email writing more effective and easier:

- **Use formal language:** Emails are mostly used for formal communication. It is important to use appropriate language and avoid informal words and slang. It does not sound serious and can make your emails appear unimportant.
- **Effective subject line:** Subject of email carries the essence of your entire email and it makes filtering out of emails easy. So it is important to write the most accurate subject line while writing an email. Your subject line should clearly convey the central topic of your email.
- **CC and BCC:** One must have seen the categories of CC and BCC in an email. These two are two different categories of the recipients of your email apart from the receiver whom the email addresses. CC stands for carbon copy and BCC stands for blind carbon copy. Both CC and BCC are not primarily addressed by the email so they do not have to respond to it. The purpose of using these categories is to send the copy of your email to others. While

the email address of CC recipient is visible to other recipients as well, in BCC the recipient's address is hidden from the rest of the recipients of the email.

- **Body of the email:** Similar to a formal letter, the main body of your mail should explain your concern concisely, clearly and briefly. Make sure you include all the important details but avoid adding any unimportant additional information which makes your emails unnecessarily lengthy.

- **Closing the email:** It is important to always end your email with a thank you note. You can use phrases such as- "looking forward to your response", "I would be grateful for your help" or "kindly look into the matter". These phrases add a formal and polite tone to your email.

- **Other important details:** Make sure to add your name at the end of the email. You can use words like, "Regards (your name)". It is important to add your designation and the institution/company you are affiliated with right below your name. Additionally, you can also include your mobile number so your receiver can reach out to you in case of some emergency.

In the book *English for Business Communication,* Mable Chan mentions some of the important techniques to use to make your emails more effective:

1. Use a descriptive subject line
2. Be concise
3. Note the formality of email & write accordingly
4. Use reminders tactfully

These points must be kept in mind while writing any email.

Now, let us look at some examples of professional e-mails.

Question:

Write an email to your boss, the Planning Head of Planning Department in your company using the below stated lines:

Learnt that boss is taking up a new project——planned for investment of 2 crore Rupees in IT——unfortunately plan will not work——competitor has similar project——this project was a failure——no demand in the market——hence should stop this idea immediately.

Answer:

Subject - <u>Urgent: Project Evaluation & Review</u>

Dear Sir,
Greetings!

This is regarding the new IT investment project that the company is considering. It is understood that the company is venturing into a major investment plan worth 2 crore Rupees in the IT Sector.

It appears that while there was initial enthusiasm on this project, our competitor has already launched a similar initiative that proved to be a failure. One of the reasons ascribed to this is the lack of market demand. Given this situation, it would be prudent to halt this investment plan as of now and wait for more clarity.

Please let me know your thoughts on this and if I can assist you in any way.

Best Regards

Aditya K. Bhardwaj
Junior Secretary
Planning Department

Take a look at another way in which the email could be written:

Subject - <u>Urgent Feedback reg. new 'IT Investment Project'</u>

Dear Sir,
Greetings of the day!

I recently learned about the new project the agency is considering, which involves a huge investment of over 2 crore Rupees in the IT sector. After giving it some thought and conducting some fact-finding research, I wanted to share some concerns that I believe are important to address before moving forward.

It appears that several competitors have similar projects in development, which could saturate the market by the time our project is completed. Secondly, there currently seems to be little to no demand for this type of project in the market.

Given these points, I strongly recommend reconsidering the project. I'm happy to discuss this in more detail if you think it would be helpful.

Best Regards

Aditya K. Bhardwaj
Junior Secretary
Planning Department

Explanation:

So, basically you have to write an email using those sentences mentioned above. You can improvise a bit and use your own phrases too. But overall the above mentioned sentences have to be used. In professional space, often we have to write mails with scant information and upon dictation only. So, in such a case it is important that we know how to write an email by using only a few sentences. In such a case, there is a need to improvise on the spot and come up with novel ways to write a professional mail.

Question:

> "Email marketing should be brief – short enough that you're able to read it on your cell phone without scrolling."
> -Dan Griffith

Write an email to the HR Head, Recruitment Unit of your firm recommending a friend for a vacant post using the below stated lines:

Recommending——my friend Amrita Sehgal——vacant post——Programmer Analyst——suitable degree——work experience——pleasant person——good addition—— team——resume

Answer:

Subject: <u>Recommending Ms. Sehgal for vacant Programmer Analyst Post</u>

Greetings!

I am writing in connection with the post of Programmer Analyst which is currently lying vacant. I would like to recommend Ms. Amrita Sehgal, a fellow former co-worker with whom I have worked at Infosys Ltd. previously.

Ms. Sehgal has a suitable degree in B.Tech from IIT-Delhi and is a Program software expert. With a pleasant personality and team spirit, I believe she can be a good addition to our agency. Please let me know if you need any clarification on this.

PFA the Resume for your kind perusal.

Best

Dr. Tridha Dutta
Executive Assistant
Programme Department

Explanation:

So, basically you have to write an email using those sentences mentioned above. You can improvise a bit and use your own phrases too. But overall the above mentioned sentences have to be used. In professional space, often we have to write mails with scant information and upon dictation only. So, in such a case it is important that we know how to write an email by using only a few sentences. In such a case, there is a need to improvise on the spot and come up with novel ways to write a professional mail.

Question:

Using the following phrases, write an email with a minimum of 120 words to a company requesting them to sponsor your college cultural festival.

reputed institute – 10 days – 200 college – cultural event – sparkling performance – extravaganza – sponsor the event – brand exposure – youth – request appointment – brochure attached

Answer:

Subject – <u>Sponsorship/ Collaboration Opportunities at HRC Cultural Festival' 24</u>

Hello!
Greetings from *Confluence' 24*

We are putting together our 15th College Cultural Festival, *Confluence' 24*, and we at Hans Raj College believe that it's something *Mama-Earth Ltd.* would be really into.

This event includes participation of 200 colleges with sparkling performances by young students and artists from all across India in this 10-Day long cultural extravaganza to be held at Hans Raj College, a reputed institution. The estimated footfall will be close to 1 million students across the universities in India.

We have crafted a range of sponsorship packages to suit different goals and budgets, ranging from 'Title Sponsor' to 'Associate/ Presenting Sponsor'. Apart from access to targeted student database and brand exposure, *Mama Earth Ltd.* will become a part of a

thriving young community. Looking forward to an appointment to discuss this more in person and to take it further from here.
PFA the detailed brochure for more details.

Ankita N.
Cultural Secretary
Hans Raj College
University of Delhi
cult_sec@hrc.edu.ac.in

Explanation:

You must have noticed that the language used in this email is strikingly different from the other examples mentioned above. The language used in this example is a mix of formal and informal both. It is done keeping in mind the informal event, i.e., organization of a cultural event at a college. So, the students can send such an email with slightly informal language. However, due diligence must be practiced to ensure that such a language is used only in cases where it suits the most. For instance, we cannot write informally when applying for a job or for any other professional communication.

Summary

This unit is dedicated to digital communication that takes place through the medium of the internet. In this unit we learned about multiple types of social media like Twitter and ways to increase your visibility and engage the audience.

Nowadays social media serves as an easy and simple way to earn money as well. Various platforms and websites provide the options of creating blogs and publishing book reviews which you can even monetize. This unit taught us how to utilize social media and the digital sphere to monetize our skills. The unit taught various methods of blog writing along with the examples of websites where you can try this. We also learned how to write book reviews along with practical examples and tips and tricks to make it easier.

Digital communication in the professional sphere is incomplete without using the platform for work and job purposes. The Internet is one of the best mediums to hunt for a job of your desires. There are multiple websites which help you create profiles and find suitable jobs and connect with recruiters. This unit taught us one of the most important professional skills of creating an academic or job profile on LinkedIn and simplified its use.

The Internet is also commonly used for learning purposes. The unit taught us how we can make the most of it by improving our note-taking and audio-book listening skills. Nowadays, there are plenty of online courses available on the internet which are a great source of learning and gaining knowledge at your own pace and from the comfort of your home. In order to make the most of these sources it is imperative to master audio book listening and note taking skills which we learned in this unit.

The unit focused on one of the most important things to know while using internet and digital platforms i.e. netiquettes. Netiquettes means the etiquettes used on the internet. They are the ways and mannerisms in which we should behave on the internet, respecting others and at the same time keeping ourselves safe from any types of hazards such as unintentional leakage of data, scams, and bullies. In this unit we learned these skills which are significant in daily use as well.

In this unit we learned about the most commonly used way of communication in the digital sphere – emails. This unit taught us the significance of email and how to write emails for professional communication. In this unit we learned with the examples of multiple emails written for various purposes. The examples were written keeping in mind demands of a professional work space.

Glossary

Abbreviation – Short form of some term, title, or words, mostly written by using the initial letter. For example, FB for Facebook.

Academic/work profile – An account of your work or academic details which shows your achievements, experiences, and the current position in your work or academic year.

Audio book – Books which are recorded by reading out loud to be listened to instead of being read.

Bio – A brief introduction of oneself on social media to be put on their social media profile. It usually includes your city, college or workplace name.

Ethnography – Ethnography is a research method used in social sciences, particularly anthropology, where researchers immerse themselves in the culture and daily lives of a group of people to understand their perspectives, behaviour, and social structures. It involves participant observation, where the researcher actively participates in the community being studied while also observing and documenting their activities and interactions.

GIF – Graphics Interchange Format. It includes short graphics and visuals used on the internet.

Keywords – Words which carry the essence of a work and commonly occur in it.

Netiquettes – Etiquettes used on the internet. These are the ways and manners in which we should behave online.

Notes – Hand-written or digitalized collection of words or information written quickly to be revisited later.

Rating – A number-based data to denote the viewership of a particular work based on its popularity.

Review – To look at something again in order to improve it or make changes. It is also used to share one's opinions or thoughts about a particular work, for example- a book review or a movie review.

URL – Uniform Resource Locator. It is the digital address of any content you find online.

Self-Assessment Questions

1. What are the effective ways of doing ethnography?
2. What is field note taking?
3. What is the difference between primary and secondary data?
4. Name a few famous ethnographies and outline their importance?
5. Define digital Divide.
6. What is data privacy and how does it protect individuals from internet-based crimes?

References

Winters, Charles, and Cotillions, National League of. E-Etiquette: The Definitive Guide to Proper Manners in Today's Digital World. United States, Skyhorse, 2015.

Berlatsky, Noah. Netiquette and Online Ethics. United States, Greenhaven Press, 2013.

Harrison, Anthony Kwame. Ethnography. United Kingdom, Oxford University Press, 2018.

Sharma, Kalindi. "The Art of Writing Field notes in 21st Century." *Ethnography and Fieldwork: Foundations of Qualitative Research.* Ed. PC Joshi and Oinam Hemlata urfat Anjem Mir. Delhi: The Readers Paradise, 2024. 65-88. 2024.

Suggested Readings

Del Vecchio, Ray (2021). *How to Start a Blog with Word Press: Beginner's Guide to Make Money by Writing Online*

Dev, A.N, Marwah, A. & Pal, Swati. (2009). *Creative Writing: A Beginner's Manual,* University of Delhi, Pearson Longman.

Schwab, Victor (1962). *How to Write a Good Advertisement*, New York. Harper & Row Publishers.

Taylor, Shirley (2012). *Model Business Letters, Emails and Other Business Documents*, Edinburgh. Pearson Education.

Unit 3
Core Professional Communication Skills

Learning Objectives

This section is about the different writing skills used in an organisation which can be categorised as core professional communication skills. These writing skills will help you in maintaining a professional outlook and help you advance in your career. The aim is to develop writing techniques that can aid a student in their professional lives. We live in a world where making a living out of writing is an option with endless opportunities and scope. This unit is written with an intention to create a study material which will help in developing techniques that can aid a student in their professional lives.

The objective of this unit is to give some practical skills to the students which they can use in their day to day lives to gain hand-on skills. Also, it is expected that students can gain first-hand experience of the job market and what to expect in a professional setting.

Introduction

In this section we will understand the various writing skills that are a part and parcel of written professional communications.

Making meaningful summaries and paraphrasing are important forms of professional communication in an organisation. In this section we will be learning how to make summaries and how to paraphrase a given text through solved examples. We will also be learning how to write professional reports and other forms of internal communication like letters, memos, office orders, minutes of meetings, etc. All these are crucial elements of what can be broadly termed as written professional communications.

It is interesting to note that professional reports, official letters, memos, office orders, minutes of meetings, etc. are forms of business correspondences which are now increasingly being used and propagated through online platforms. Nowadays, these aforementioned communications are conveyed through mail, or through the websites of the organisation issuing them. But traditionally, they have always been used in manual terms and for the sake of convenience they have been categorised in this section. Memos and office orders even today are displayed prominently on the notice boards of various organisations and still continue to spread information to all stakeholders within an organisation. Minutes of meetings even today are taken down by a member in a meeting who is entrusted with the responsibility of noting down the proceedings of a particular meeting while it is getting conducted. But it is equally true that these forms of professional correspondences are progressively taking a centre stage in digital modes as well. Despite these forms of communication rapidly shifting towards digital mode, they still hold a significant place in professional communication and writing skills. From the beginning of time the idea of noting down has been conveyed through written form and professional correspondence also is in many ways associated with this idea.

Art of Writing Summary

Summarising is the art of shortening lengthy messages. If you know how to adequately summarise any topic or sentence then it shows that you can articulate your thoughts easily. The art of summarising can be helpful in discussions, writing answers, and what not. It will be helpful in areas apart from academics too. Even in academics the art of summarising can actually help you write crisp answers which will ultimately add to your academic excellence.

In Business Communication we tend to be in a situation which demands rapidly taking down summaries of certain events, meetings, functions, and even extensive write-ups. Summarising is an essential writing skill and is used in professional settings to save time. The shorter you communicate and the more precise it is, the better you can communicate in a professional setting. This sense of brevity will then ultimately add to your communication skills. The purpose of this module is to learn communication in professional life and therefore to enhance professional communication skills. Hence, we need to study how to effectively summarise lengthy messages so as to convey our viewpoint in the shortest manner possible. But first let us first understand the importance of summary writing.

Importance of Summary

- A properly laid out summary can be an essential time saver as we can read a summarised version faster and more efficiently over a larger text.
- A summary makes it easy to understand important points in a larger document, the key details in the document. This ultimately makes it easily understandable.
- Capsule summaries are a brisk and tidy method of writing which makes revision easier.
- Practicing summary writing improves one's communication and comprehension skills in general and writing skills in particular.
- A good summary can help a reader to focus only on the major thrust area of a larger text and thereby leave out minor or less important details.

We live today in a world of information overload. In such times, summarizing is an underrated skill that is extremely crucial for efficient communication. Now, since we have understood the need and benefits of summary, let us look at some points which need to be kept in mind while attempting to write a summary.

> "Perhaps the best test of a man's intelligence is his capacity for making a summary."
> -Lytton Strachey

How to write a Summary?

- A summary must convey the original idea in the same way as the original text.

- A summary is usually one-third the length of the original text. For instance, if the given passage is of 150 words, then you have to wrap it up in 50 words or so. Do not exceed 70 words in any case.

- To put it in other words, for roughly 3-4 lines of the original text, you must make one line for final summary. Summarise the given text in parts.

- Focus on the lines where the author is laying stress. Try to find the crux of the essay. Find the main argument of the essay. This step is known as close reading.

- You must identify the key point of the original text. This is the most important step and this point must be mentioned in the final summary. Your final summary should contain this point.

- Avoid points which are not there in the original text. Restrict yourself only to the original text. Your final summary should include only those points which are there in the original text.

- Combine multiple sentences into one. Use conjunction words (such as 'and', 'or', 'but', 'nor' etc.) which can be used to connect words and phrases.

- Unnecessary words like quotes, data, facts, etc. can be avoided in the final summary.

- Avoid repetitive phrases and sentences which seem redundant because the main aim is to shorten the text from its original length.

- Write in abbreviations only where possible. Use commonly accepted abbreviations only.

- First create a larger draft, then edit it further to shorten the text and minimise it. This is because larger text can be made shorter easily but smaller text requires more efforts to lengthen it.

- Always remember to put the name of the title and other details on the top before writing down a summary.

- Summary has no fixed format. It is not absolute. It can be written in any way but keeping the above points in mind while writing will ensure accuracy and ease of writing down a summary.

Practice
Q1. What are the key benefits of writing a summary?
Q2. What are the important rules to follow while writing a summary?

Let us now try to understand how to summarize effectively through some solved examples.

Example 1
Passage:

Pure water is considered as one that contains all essential chemical elements and minerals of water at levels which do not pose risk to health. Absolutely pure water is not found in nature. Actually, deionized distilled water is undesirable for health. Certain salts and gases in solution make water more palatable if not present in excess. Many of the chemicals and substances may be naturally occurring in water but the concentration is the key factor in distinguishing between a natural component and contaminant. Being an excellent solvent, groundwater can contain lots of dissolved chemicals. The ground has an excellent mechanism for filtering out particulate matter, but the dissolved chemicals and gases can still occur in large enough concentration in groundwater to cause pollution. Like surface water, groundwater resources are vulnerable to contamination from many human activities. For example, from animal waste, fertilisers, herbicides, insecticides and fungicides etc. are applied to cropland, some may leach into the groundwater resources. (**158 words**)

> **Summary:**
> Pure water contains some chemicals and minerals in limited quantity. The concentration decides whether it is natural component or a contaminant. Contaminants can be natural or human induced. Natural contaminants can originate from rocks and soil whereas human induced contaminants, like fertilizers, herbicides, etc. leach into groundwater and contaminate it.
> **(50 words)**

Explanation:

The focus area or the most important line or the crux of the passage can be said to lie in the line 'concentration is the key factor in distinguishing between a natural component and contaminant.'

Hence, it can be seen that in the summary above, this point is mentioned. Always remember to put those points in the final summary which are important and which form the crux of the essay. If you do not put it in the summary then you would not be effective enough in your answer.

Example 2
Passage:

Recycling is the process of converting waste material into new product. The product can be same or some other material. It helps in reducing the consumption of energy, fresh raw material, air and water pollution. There are many materials which are recyclable in nature lying around us. Recyclable material includes glass, paper, metals, plastic, clothes, electronic goods and so on. Recycling helps in reducing the use of natural resources. For e.g., paper is produced from the bark of trees. The recycling of paper reduces the consumption of the bark. It also saves energy, as less energy is required in recycling as compared to the production of fresh raw material. It also decreases environmental pollution. However, every material cannot be recycled, but recycling reduces the burden of natural resources, saves energy, and decreases environmental pollution. It is economic as well as beneficial for us. It is our responsibility to use recyclable material in place of non-recyclable material. (**156 words**)

Summary:

Recycling means converting waste into new products. Glass, paper, metal, plastic, clothes etc. are recyclable materials. Paper recycling reduces use of natural resources, barks of trees, energy and pollution. We must use recyclable material in place of non-recyclable material to save energy and decrease pollution. It is our responsibility to use recyclable materials. (**53 words**)

Art of Writing Paraphrase

In the previous part we studied the topic Summary and ways to write a good summary. We studied that summarizing is the art of shortening a lengthy passage. We also understood the importance of summarizing and writing with precision and in a brisk manner with some solved examples. In this section, we will study the topic paraphrasing and will try to understand its importance in a professional setting. We will also study the differences between Summary and Paraphrase and will then try to understand it with the help of some solved examples.

Summarizing and Paraphrasing are very similar in their essence, so much so that one may confuse one with the other. However, summary is the shortened version of the source material. Paraphrasing, on the other hand means restating the original text in a different form than that of the original text. Hence, this means that paraphrasing is not concerned with the length. In the previous part we studied that a summary is usually $1/3^{rd}$ of its original text. But when it comes to paraphrasing, we do not need to follow any such length related rules.

Moreover, we can improvise in a paraphrase by adding words but not in a summary. Another major difference between a summary and paraphrase is that a summary usually contains the main and key points of a larger text. A paraphrase however, contains all the details in a reworded or re-phrased manner.

Importance of Paraphrasing

- One of the main benefits of paraphrasing is that it allows us to better understand a given text in our own words.

- Effective paraphrasing is an important writing skill in the field of higher education as it is an important research skill. For writing research papers, dissertations and theses, a research scholar needs to have good paraphrasing skills.

- Effective paraphrasing leads us to inculcate a habit of original writing and communication and promotes creativity as well.

- It is also an equally useful writing skill for writing blogs and books. Overall, it improves our comprehension skills.

- In a professional setting, paraphrasing can be a useful technique while conducting group projects, writing group reports and documenting important paperwork.

> "Inevitably, almost everything we say is either quotation or paraphrase."
> -Mason Cooley

How to Paraphrase a Text?

- A Paraphrase needs not be shorter than its original text. It can be of the exact length as well as a bit longer than that.

- Paraphrase involves rephrasing the passage and hence you can use a huge amount of leverage and freedom and improvisation to write your answer.

- You can also use synonyms to replace the original words.

- One of the best ways to write a good paraphrase is to first fully understand the meaning of the original text and then write it in your own way.

- Find the original idea, the unique idea of the text and that must be mentioned in the final paraphrase as well.

- You may also start the paraphrase with a general statement other than the one mentioned in the original text. It can be a general statement of a general nature which can be used anywhere.

- You can always rephrase a statement in a different manner than what was written earlier on. You can change the order of the words to do this.

- Active voice can also be converted to passive voice. This is also an acceptable form of paraphrase though it should not be overdone.

- In a paraphrase, you may also add some real-life examples to make your point clearer. Any extra information or additional information can be added in a paraphrase. Hence, you can improvise in a paraphrase as per the need of the question.

- Paraphrase involves extending the length of the original text but that does not necessarily mean excessive lengths. If the original text is of 50 words, then do not exceed 70 words in the answer at any cost. Doing so would be incorrect.

Practice
Q1. What do you understand by the term 'paraphrasing'?
Q2. What are the major uses of paraphrasing in professional life?
Q3. How do you differentiate paraphrasing from summary?

Example 1
Passage

Success is a difficult term to define. It can't be measured in physical dimensions and given a specific meaning. Success to one person can't be viewed as success to another. Some of the persons take it as fulfilment of dream, but different people have different dreams. For example, if one dreams of acquiring enormous wealth and becomes wealthy: it is her/his personal achievement. Wealth does not guarantee success. One can also be successful without wealth. Some other dreams of getting higher education and fulfils the dream; it is her/his academic success. But if s/he fails to secure a suitable employment, her/his success may be taken as failure.

> **Paraphrase:**
> Success has a lot of meanings. It may mean different for different people and can change according to one's preference. There are people for whom gaining a lot of wealth means success. But this does not mean that it is the exact meaning of success. Different people have different dreams and the meaning of success is different for them. There are people who can be happy and contended even without huge amount of wealth and they can still be successful. Similarly, some dream of getting good marks in academics and that is success for them. But it does not mean that success only means getting high grades. Hence, success cannot be measured in physical dimensions or in a rigid manner.

Explanation:

Reading the first 4-5 lines of the original text, one gets the impression that the passage is about the different meanings of success and that the passage goes on to explain what success means differently to different people and situations. Hence, the line "Success has a lot of meanings" is mentioned right at the beginning of the Paraphrase. This is the original idea of the text.

In the above Paraphrase we have tried to understand the original idea of the text and rephrased it in a different manner. We can also improvise wherever necessary. At the same time, we have taken sentences from the original text and rephrased it in a different manner. This is how you write a correct Paraphrase.

Example 2
Passage

Ragging is the harassment of new coming students by the senior students of same institution. It involves physical, mental, psychological or sexual harassment of newcomers. It is a damaging form of interaction. It is meant to make newcomers familiar with their seniors and inject confidence among them, but it has become a menace in educational institutions. Some senior students tease, torment, and even rough up the newcomers under the excuse of 'introduction' which generates fear among them. Sometimes it starts with harmless leg pulling and goes to harsh physical and mental assault. It is the latter type of ragging that is objectionable and matter of great concern. It often takes a malignant form wherein the newcomers are subjected to physical or psychological torture which leaves an indelible unpleasant scar in victim's mind and haunts her/him for years. There are numerous cases where people have lost their mental balance or committed suicide. Many a times, the students, succumb to ragging, drop out, thereby hampering their career prospects. There are cases of may bright students whose careers have been ruined because of ragging.

Paraphrase

Ragging is the act of senior students at the same institution harassing newcomers. It involves newcomers being mentally, psychologically, sexually and even physically harassed. The interaction can be quite distressing and damaging. It aims to make newcomers feel familiar with their surroundings and trust the seniors, but in educational institutions it has taken up an ugly face now. In the garb of 'Introduction', some senior students tease, torture and even trouble the newcomers which generates fear amongst them. It can start with a harmless leg pull and progress to physical and mental abuse. The latter type of ragging is notably objectionable and a cause of concern. It frequently takes a harmful form in which newcomers are made to go through psychological torture, leaving an unpleasant scar on the victim's mind that can linger for years. It can leave him/ her shattered. There are various examples of ragging victims losing their mental peace or committing suicide because they were unable to bear the unimaginable pain and shock from their mental torture. Students even frequently drop out from their colleges, thus jeopardising their careers and ruining their futures. Many brilliant students have had their careers destroyed as a result of ragging.

To gain an even better understanding of how to write a paraphrase, let us look at another example of a paraphrase for the same passage given earlier on. Notice that this is very similar but written in an entirely different manner.

> **Paraphrase**
>
> The harassment or torture of fresher students by the seniors of the same institution is termed as 'ragging'. Earlier it was done as sort of introduction to newcomers to familiarise them with seniors and instil confidence in them. But now, due to involvement of teasing, torture, bullying and other damaging interactions, it has become a menace. It generally proceeds with harmless leg pulling but in no time reaches to harsh physical and mental torment. Harsh ragging can lead to destruction of mental peace of the victim. There have been cases when the victims unable to bear the pain and shock of physical and mental harassment have lost their mental balance and have even took their own lives. Often students drop out of their education and this leads to a ruined career prospect for them. Ragging is matter of concern as it hampers the future of students and there have been several instances of such students losing out on their careers.

Letter Writing

In the current part, we will learn about Formal Business Letters or Application Letters and the techniques on how to write Formal Letters.

Formal Letters

Formal letters, as the name suggests are very formal in nature and are those which are sent for official purposes.

Format for writing a Formal Letter –

Writer's address
Date of writing the letter
Recipient's address
Salutation
Subject (in maximum 2 lines)
Body: (In 2 or maximum 3 paragraphs)
Signature/ Designation

Some points to be kept in mind while attempting this kind of letter:

1.   Always write in a simple, easy to understand language which is comprehensible to one and all. Do not use flowery and highly embellished language, except for some official terms.

2.   In this type of letter, you cannot use language freely like you did in an informal letter.

3.   Do not use colloquial, day-to-day language and informal words like 'Hey', 'Hi', 'Whats'up', etc. These words must never be used at any cost as you have to make the letter sound formal and serious in nature.

4.   Be formal, to the point, stern and restrained in speech.

5.   Follow a tripartite structure (which includes 3 parts of a letter – intro, main body, conclusion).

6.   Use words which are formal in nature. Words such as 'looking forward to', 'would be obliged', 'please expedite the matter', 'this is to inform you', 'this is to bring to your notice', 'through the columns of your esteemed newspaper' etc. can be used.

7.   Word limit: around 150-200 words. Formal letters can be a bit lengthier as well, depending on the business context. So, you have the liberty to write extensively.

You can find below a formal letter for your reference. This is a letter to the editor of a newspaper.

101- C New Colony,
Sarita Vihar, Block 1,
New Delhi- 110076.

24th July 2025

The Chief Editor,
New Delhi Times, Delhi,
Delhi- 110023.

Respected sir/ ma'am

<u>**Subject**</u> – <u>Problem of eve teasing and lack of surveillance in the society</u>

I would kindly like to draw your attention to the issue of the constant eve teasing and its continuity in our society. Women and girls of our society have been facing this issue for a month now. There is a group of boys who do not belong to our society but they have been visiting the public park in our society. They outrage the modesty of the women by catcalling them and using vulgar words and gestures. This park is a public property and belongs to the people of the society but because of these anti-social elements it has become the centre of abuse. Women of our society do not feel safe in the place they belong to. Their daily life is interrupted and disturbed because of this.

Despite our complaint to the local police station and a request to set CCTV cameras for safety measures, no response has been received by us for two weeks. Our demand is that strict actions should be taken against these boys and CCTV cameras should be installed in the society as a step towards safety by surveillance to avoid the entry of such people who pollute the environment of our society.

On behalf of our society, I request you to kindly look into the matter and raise our issue through your esteemed newspaper to draw the attention of the concerned authorities to our problem. We would be grateful to you for your much needed help. We are also open to any kind of interaction with you if required for the purpose of your report. I am looking forward to hearing from you.

Thank you.

Yours truly
Alka

Business Letters

Some standard practices and points which may be used across all sorts of formal applications or business letters are:

1.   Reference should be given about any previous contact in the beginning. References are important in a business letter which also explain the background of the letter being written. You may use sentences such as "This is in reference to your letter dated..." or "With regard to your memo dated..." or "With reference to your letter dated..."

2.   Business letters usually contain a reference to the future too. This is mostly given at the end. In other words, this means asking for action from the recipient.

3.   In the opening, if you do not know the name of the receiver, then you can use 'Dear Sir/Ma'am' as opening.

4.   Always write the letter in first person only. Use either 'I' or 'We'. Use 'We' if writing on behalf of your company.

5.   End the letter on a cordial note with a positive tone. You may use sentences such as, "Thank you for your interest in the company", or "We take this opportunity to thank you for..." or "Please do not hesitate to get in touch with our representative", "We look forward to hearing from you" etc.

> "Letters are among the most significant memorial a person can leave behind them."
> -Johann Wolfgang von Goethe

Report Writing

Reports are one of the most essential forms of business correspondences. This is because writing a report is a central aspect of any business and professional communication. Report writing is an essential business skill as it is used everywhere. From newspapers, press houses, to government agencies and private firms – a report is written everywhere.

First of all, let us see what a Report actually is. The word "report" has been derived from the Latin *'reportare'* which means to 'bring back'. Hence, this makes it amply clear that we need to recollect or bring back the events. This is what a report means – to report activities and present them as they happened.

A report can be the description of an event by a person who witnessed it to somebody else who was not present on the scene. A report is a formal document written for a specific audience to meet a specific need. It may contain facts of a situation, project and process; an analysis and interpretation of data, events and records; conclusions drawn from objective data or suggestion and recommendations.

Some points to be kept in mind while writing Reports –

• There is always a need to first prepare your material before writing down a report. You must know the objective and readership before writing a report.

• You must collect the material that has to be included in the report. Select only relevant material. You need to hence create a broad skeletal framework before writing a report. All these steps constitute the planning of the report.

• Reports are objective in nature and therefore should contain facts. Facts should be related to the event in question and must be accurate. Facts are the most important part of any report.

• Reports are mostly investigative in nature; hence there is a need to put new findings in it.

• Use simple language, free from any technical jargon. Simpler the language, the better it is.

• Use past tense in writing a report as you are writing about events that have already happened and belong to the past.

• Always be highly objective in writing a report. Do not be subjective or write your own personal views. Your own biases, emotions etc. must find no place in the report. Be objective.

• Towards the end provide recommendations and suggestions. This is very important in those reports which ask you to investigate into some matter of urgency.

- The layouts should always be uniform. While writing dates you may use dd/mm/yyyy format as it is the most commonly acceptable form. But whichever format you use, it should be consistent throughout.

- Headings, sub-headings, paragraphs and pages should always have a uniform layout. Do not change layout as it looks unprofessional and untidy.

- Avoid writing too many facts without explanation. Only relevant and meaningful facts should be there in a report with proper logic and explanation to back it up.

---

4 Most Important Points –

   i.   You have to report the events and happenings as they happened with facts.

   ii.   Analyse the situation.

   iii.   Describe the cause of the problem by giving reasons for it.

   iv.   Give suggestions or recommendations.

Characteristics of a Good Report –

1. Precision: Effective report must clearly reflect its purpose. It must not be ambiguous.

2. Factual details: The report should be very detailed and factual. Try to put facts in it related to the question asked. But it must not be irrelevant to the question.

3. Simple and unambiguous language: A good report should be written in simple and unambiguous language. It should be clear, brief and grammatically correct.

4. There should be a properly laid out conclusion at the end. There should also be recommendations at the end.

5. It is better to give summary of the entire report at the end. It makes it more professional. This summary must be there in the analytical report

Practice

Q1. Explain the use and significance of Reports in professional correspondence.

Q2. Write a detailed report of any cultural activity held in your college/ institution/ school/ firm.

Q3. What are the characteristics of a good report?

Format/ Types of Reports

Letter Format: This format may be used for short reports that have to be communicated to someone outside the organization. E.g., giving report of activities of college to the Vice-Chancellor of the University. It is a report in the form of a letter and hence needs to be written as per the Letter Format.

Format of a Letter Report

REPORT WRITER'S ADDRESS
REFERENCE NO. (optional)

DATE
RECEIVER'S ADDRESS
SUBJECT
SALUTATION
CONTENT:
Introduction (context/ background)
Findings (supporting text with all findings, facts, information etc.)
Conclusion (with recommendations, solutions etc.)

COMPLIMENTARY CLOSE
SIGNATURE
YOUR NAME

Memo Format: This format may be used for short reports that have to be communicated to someone within the organization. It is meant for internal communication. E.g. – sending information to a senior within an organization, providing investigations into any problem, providing solutions to a problem, writing a report on activities of a college to the Principal of the college.

Remember that you have to mention as many facts as possible when you are reporting an event that happened in your college. Since the report is to be submitted to the Principal of your college, hence it means that it is to be written within an organization. Therefore, you have to follow the Memo Format for writing this type of Report.

Format of a Memo Report

<table>
<tr><td>

ADDRESS
INTEROFFICE MEMORANDUM/ REPORT
DATE:
TO:
FROM:
SUBJECT:

CONTENT:

Introduction (context/ background)
Findings (supporting text with all findings, facts, information etc.)
Conclusion (with recommendations, solutions etc.)

COMPLIMENTARY CLOSE
SIGNATURE
YOUR NAME

</td></tr>
</table>

> "All a company report and balance sheet can tell you is the past and the present. They cannot tell future."
> -Nikolas Darvas

> ## Any report should contain 3 major heads –
>
> 1. **Introduction** - In the Introduction, you need to introduce the topic and the subject matter of the report with clarity and conciseness. You can begin by saying who asked you to write the report and what task you have undertaken. You can give the objective of the report in the introduction and even discuss the importance of a report.
>
> 2. **Main body** - Next comes the main head of your report, ie Findings. Under this you have to present all your data, facts, pie-charts, figures and data in a manner which explains your thesis. If it is an analytical/ interpretative report then there is a need to give proper justification and explanation for the facts mentioned. this should be done in the main body.
>
> 3. **Conclusion** – The last section is conclusion. This should contain a very brief summary of whatever has been achieved in the report till now. In other words, you may write the result of the report in this part. The summary should explain in an easy manner the findings of the report. Also, this section should contain some recommendations at the end. Always ensure that the conclusion flows naturally from the findings and the results. Any other appendices, if any, may be attached at the end. Sources or references, if any, may be attached at the end. It is important to note that appendixes and sources are optional.

Types of Reports

Broadly we will discuss two types of report which are most frequently used in business communications –

Project Report

When one completes a particular research or development project, one needs to prepare a completion report. This completion report is called a project report. The main function of a project report is to give the individual, organization, institution or a company an accounting of the project completed. It is a systematic presentation and discussion of the data collected and analysed as a part of project. It can also be called as informational reports.

Progress reports, instructional reports, informative reports and research reports are the types which fall under this category.

It usually presents researched data and is a result of a project undertaken by the company. These types of reports are very targeted in nature. They are also highly objective and rely solely on facts and data.

Analytical Report

Analytical reports are usually done to investigate into something. They are written to analyse a situation or a new development in a business environment. Analytical reports, as the name suggests are analytical in nature, i.e., there is a need to search for new findings in it. Analytical reports can also be called as Interpretative reports.

Usually, such reports give a conclusion or highlight new developments in a field. They aid in research and better planning within an organisation. Government agencies, NGOs, scientific organisations also write analytical reports which can help them develop better welfare schemes. Also, these types of reports are used to investigate the financial affairs of a company. System evaluation reports, technical reports and trouble-shooting reports are the types which fall under this category.

Analytical reports are mostly subjective in nature as they are analysed and written by a business professional.

Importance of reports/ why do we need to write reports?
- → To find research findings/ results
- → To analyse the results for policy and other decision-making processes
- → To present and organise data and facts related to some event for future reference
- → To investigate into some matter related to business and organisational value
- → To give recommendations based on proper analysis and research

---

Example:

Dr. Pooja Goswami, HoD of Humanities Department has been asked by the Education Ministry to conduct a survey of college students at her college to find out what kind of education they think will be the most valuable to them at the college level. Write a **<u>Report</u>** of your findings and your proposals for action to the Education Minister. Also, give some suggestions at the end of the Report.

REPORT
JOHN F. KENNEDY COLLEGE
Jeevan Bhagwan Nagar, Delhi – 11065

Date: 18th September 2025
To: Ministry of Education, GoI
From: Dr. Pooja Goswami
Sub: <u>Investigative Survey to Propose Appropriate & Innovative Pedagogical Techniques for Higher Education</u>

After thorough talks & survey directions provided by the Ministry of Education, a survey was conducted in the college to find out what kind of education system students believe would be most valuable for them at college level.

<u>Following findings were found</u>:

1. **Frequency of Practicals**: College has advanced and modern practical labs with good accommodation capacity. However, compared to this, the number of practicals conducted are quite less. All students get a chance of performing one practical only once.

2. **Attendance & Other Activities**: Students who are enrolled in various co-curricular societies of the college often struggle with their attendance although they are quite good at their studies and represent college to the society. Therefore, attendance benefits must be given to bona fide students who miss their class in order to contribute in such co-curricular exercises.

3. **Career Counselling**: Most of the students especially the new first year students often struggle with their carrier options as they are new to course and no idea about it and they are mostly confused.

4. **Workshops**: Workshops should be conducted to provide exposure to real life situations. More and more practical work should be conducted at these workshops.

5. **Special Compulsory Courses**: Some special compulsory courses should be introduced to enhance students' skills. These courses should include ancillary knowledge which is must for real life professional situations.

Recommendations: Current education system is fairly effective but after the Survey following proposals can be drawn for betterment of current education system to make it more efficient:

- More practicals should be conducted for students to prepare well for coming future job and other professional opportunities.
- Attendance benefits must be given to bona fide students who miss their class in order to contribute in co-curricular exercises.
- Career guidance should be provided to the students in terms of lectures, workshops, interaction sessions, etc to provide real life exposure of situations.
- A pool of Skill Enhancement Courses (SECs) & Value Addition Courses (VACs) must be incorporated.
- Final year students should be given special sessions on campus placement and mock-interviews to be held.

Dr. Pooja Goswami
Head of Department
Humanities Department
John F. Kennedy College
0-999162969 (M)

Here is another example of an investigative Report.

Example:

You are working as a Sales Executive Manager at Honda Cars India Ltd. Recently, your company has registered ground breaking sales in the quarter III of financial year 2023-24. You have been asked to investigate into this and find the reasons for the same. Write an investigative report seeking the reasons and offer some suggestions at the end about future course of action.

HONDA CARS INDIA LTD.
Noida, Uttar Pradesh 345890

INTER-OFFICE REPORT
18th September 2025

Board of Directors
Honda Cars India Ltd.
Noida, Uttar Pradesh-345890

Sub – <u>Investigative Report on Increase in Sales, Quarter III, 2023-24</u>

The company has registered ground breaking sales and is currently running in profit in the quarter ending July 2024. After a thorough investigation and talks with the company's dealers, production managers, supervisors and dealers of other companies, a survey was carried out to know customer's responses and opinions on the increase in the company's sales. The following reasons were found for the increase:

1.   <u>Technology</u>
The company has been in the field of automobile manufacturing for the last 25 years and has been doing a great job. No other company has overtaken it so far. The reason for this is latest technology that the company has been launching.

2.   **Mileage**

Our cars have delivered better mileage than rival companies. We have been able to deliver constant mileage of 25 kmpl which is the highest among all car companies.

3.   **Models**

The company has the best of the car models in terms of design and technology. Our designing team has been coming up with facelifted versions and new designs which attract the attention of the buyers.

4.   **Price**

There is a huge competition in terms of pricing in automobile sector. But detailed surveys have shown that the cost-to-expense ratio of our cars is very less which makes it highly affordable for the buyers. We have kept prices reliable and in control. We also offer finance options to the customers.

Recommendations:

The company has been doing great till now and to keep this going there are some recommendations below:

a)   Increase in mileage of new models
b)   More attractive advertisements to be rolled out
c)   Showrooms and service centres should be increased and should be available across the city.

Vandita Dayal
Sales Executive Manager, Honda Cars India Ltd.
0-896162966 (M)

Note: To make a report look more professional you may also include a cover letter/ report cover. It acts as a cover to your report and is attached at the beginning of the report. It acts as an introduction to the report. It creates a good impression within a business sphere and gives the impression of the report being conclusive, targeted and professional in nature.

You must mention following things in your report cover -

- Name of organisation
- Title of report
- Report written by
- Report submitted to
- Date of submission

"When I was in the seventh grade, I did a report about the environment and the loss of species. It was supposed to be only a few pages, but ended up being nearly 50."
-Woody Harrelson

Example of a Report Cover –

Honda Cars India Ltd.
Noida, Uttar Pradesh 345890

<u>Investigative Report on Increase in Sales, Quarter III (2023-24)</u>

Report submitted by:
Vandita Dayal
Sales Executive Manager, Honda Cars India Ltd

Report submitted to:
Board of Directors, Honda Cars India Ltd.
18th September 2025

Other Important Terms & Definitions

Project Report:

When one completes a particular research or development project, one needs to prepare a completion report. This completion report is called a project report. The main function of a project report is to give the individual, organization, institution or a company an accounting of the project completed. It is a systematic presentation and discussion of the data collected and analysed as a part of project.

Thesis/ Dissertation:

A Thesis or Dissertation is a research report that presents research data- either original research work or information gained largely from printed information sources or from other sources. It is a written composition describing, discussing or analysing a systematic investigation towards increasing the sum of the knowledge in a specific area or field.

Memos, Office Orders, Minutes

Memos

Memos and office orders are basically forms of internal communication in a business setting. They are meant for internal correspondences and communicate vital information within an organisation. Such forms of correspondences flow downwardly from the upper hierarchical reaches to the lower ones. They do not flow upwards as memos and office orders do not demand any immediate response from the recipient.

Memos are more general in nature. Memos are issued to fulfil various needs in an organisation. Some ways in which memos are used are –

- To share any kind of information in an organisation
- To share business decisions and instructions
- To demand action on any particular event
- To seek information or suggestions from the recipients

How to Write Memos?

- You have to tell the receivers about some information. So, try to disseminate the information in a short manner.

- You may use chronological method of writing the memo by chronologically organising the information.
- Give facts in a memo and be highly objective in writing a memo. Personal opinions, biases should not be there in a memo.
- Use simple, clear and jargon-free language in a memo.
- Memos are mostly about events and information that are to be passed to the office. So, try to explain cause/ effect of any event.
- Explain briefly the reasons about any action.
- Write the memo in bullet points. Do not write in paragraphs. This is because only vital information has to be passed on to the office.

Let us look at a sample memo to understand how memos are written in a professional setting:

Havells India Limited
Choksey Towers, Gurgaon 110066
Ph. No 34567890
memo.office@havells.in.du

MEMORANDUM
Ref. no. HVLS/ 2023/ memo
29th April 2025

The Annual General Meeting (AGM) in its 198th meeting has agreed to the following –

1. That investors will be given a bonus share of the company with ratio 2:1 w.e.f. 17th Sept 2025 (ex-date).
2. Upon enquiries the AGM has decided to conduct interim audit of financial affairs of company.
3. This is for the information of all concerned office bearers.

CC-
All concerned Departments
For any queries mail on the aforementioned email address.

Office Orders

Office Orders are more specific in nature. Office order is mostly a specific response to some event in an office and usually demand swift action. Also, mostly office orders are aimed to employees or group of employees and therefore are essential form of internal communication for employees' rights.

Office Orders – Significance

- To withdraw rights of any individual in the company.
- To offer promotion to any individual.
- To take disciplinary action against any individual.
- To transfer any individual or offer alternative postings.
- To offer increment to employees or group of employees in an organisation.

How to write Office Orders?

- Always present the information in a factual manner.
- Use simple, clear and jargon-free language.
- Personal opinion, biases and views shall not be there in an office order. Be highly objective while writing an office order.
- Since office orders are targeted in approach, make sure you answer the 3 W's (Who, What, When) in it.

Havells India Limited
Choksey Towers, Gurgaon 110066
Ph. No 34567890
order.office@havells.in

OFFICE ORDER
Ref. no. HVLS/2022/order
29th April 2025

The management is pleased to inform that the recently constituted Sales Committee has published its report after a

thorough action plan implemented by them. The committee had Ms. Sonia, Ms. Priya and Mr. Ahlawat as joint members in it.
As recognition of the exceptional services of the aforementioned employees, we are happy to announce a bonus to the team in accordance with the norms stipulated by the company's AGM.

Minutes of Meetings

The notes that you make while attending a meeting are known as the minutes of meeting. They include highlighting the major issues discussed during the meeting or any voting and activities that take place during the meeting. There is usually a designation for the member who records the minutes of a meeting.

Minutes of Meetings – Significance

Minutes are an important part of professional communication for various reasons. Some of these are –

- Taking minutes of meeting is important because it works as a reminder.
- The minutes help in keeping a track of what happens in a meeting and track the activities taking place during the meeting.
- It is very helpful for future correspondences as it keeps track of the happenings in a meeting.
- In case there arises some issue in the future, these minutes of meeting can work as the evidence of what happened during the meeting.
- It helps people who were absent during the meeting to know about any important decisions and to know what happened during the meeting.

> "A meeting is an event at which the minutes are kept and the hours are lost."
> -Joseph Stilwell

How to Write Minutes of Meetings?

The following points should be kept in mind while writing Minutes of Meetings:

- One should write minutes of the meeting objectively in clear words.
- Highly technical terms and abbreviations should be avoided as they can cause confusion.
- It is advised to avoid mentioning names of each member unless it is required. The most important thing to mention are the resolutions that were made during the meeting.
- One should record the names of the members who attend the meeting as well as those who were not present.
- If there arises a need to modify minutes of meeting the changes can be made with consideration.

Minutes of Meeting

29th December 2024, 10:00 AM

A meeting was held on the aforementioned date and time by the Department of Indian Literature, University of Texas at the Board Conference Room to discuss various emergent issues related to organizational structure of the Department and to discuss future course of action.

Attendee List
- Priya Gupta
- Shanila Murtaza
- Rakesh Mehta
- Reena Roy

Absentee list
- Raghav Singh

Minutes

- Newly appointed faculty member Priya Gupta was welcomed by everyone at the Department.
- The members got to know other members of the Department and got familiar with each other.
- The structure of the Department has been made with the consideration of every member's inputs.
- Members brainstormed new ideas and concepts for curriculum development for the students at the Department.

Discussion

Department faculty members introduced themselves in order to get familiar with each other. Every faculty member provided inputs and took a position to provide a structured shape to the Department. Suggestions from every member were considered keeping in mind the future goals of the Department and to serve the requirements of students at the Department.

Adjournment

The meeting ended with a speech by the manager. As per the schedule the meeting concluded at 11:30 AM.

Next Meeting

The next meeting will take place on 29th January 2025 at 10:00 am on the same platform.

Now, let us see one more example of a Minutes of a Meeting below. This is the successive meeting of the one held above. This is another example with a different format which can allow readers to understand more fully on how to write the Minutes of a Meeting.

MINUTES OF MEETING
Departmental Meeting

Date	December 29th 2024
Time	10:00 AM
Meeting called by	Department of Indian Literature, University of Texas

In attendance:
Priya Gupta, Shanila Murtaza, Rakesh Mehta, Reena Roy, Raghav Singh

In absence:
None

Approval of Minutes:
1. The minutes were read from the August 2024 meeting and approved.
2. Reena Roy was nominated as the new Teacher-in-Charge of the Department for the academic year 2024-25. A motion to elect Roy was carried by Rakesh Mehta who is the outgoing Teacher-in-Charge for the academic year 2023-24. The motion was seconded by Raghav Singh.
3. All present voted in favor and Reena Roy was confirmed as the new Teacher-in-Charge (2024-25).

Annual Report Presentation:
Outgoing TIC Rakesh Mehta presented the Annual Department Report which included:

- Department Annual Report for Academic Year 2023-24
- Fiscal expenditure & fiscal review of upcoming academic year

- Faculty Development Programs (FDPs) for training & opportunities
- Admissions for the Academic Year 2024-25

Announcements:
Date and Venue for Departmental educational trip to Delhi Literature Festival' 2025 was confirmed. More details will come soon.

Next Meeting:
Motion to adjourn the meeting was passed unanimously and the meeting ended at 12PM with a Departmental Lunch. Next meeting will be held as per requirement and will be informed through mail to all.

The Meeting concluded with a Vote of Thanks to all.

CV/ Resume/ Bio-Data

CV/ Resume are forms of job correspondences/ business correspondences which showcases your organisational skills, achievements, experiences with an aim to highlight you as a prospective job candidate. Such forms of job correspondences are meant to make you stand out from the rest.

CV or a Resume is not just needed for jobs, but can also be used for temporary jobs, internships, voluntary works, part-time jobs, placements, etc. Overall, in almost any sphere of the job market today, we need to have a well laid out CV/ Resume to make ourselves stand out from the crowd and to emerge as a strong candidate with great management skills.

The world is now changing at a rapid pace. The need for CVs, Resume is all the more urgent now. At some point of time, all of us have to create a CV for ourselves if we need to get into the job market as potential candidates for qualified jobs. A good CV & Resume should allow a candidate to highlight himself/ herself as a qualified job applicant. It should also reflect the candidate's key strengths.

Resume

Resume originates from the French word which means summary. A Resume is hence a summary of a candidate's skills that they have gained including their education and employment. It is not as detailed as a CV as a resume is more targeted and is rather a summary of events/ achievements/ qualifications of a candidate.

A Resume should highlight the key elements required for a job and must highlight area of expertise/ area of interest, work experience, internships and other professional experiences of a candidate.

A Resume therefore is not lengthy and should be usually kept within 2 pages only. Resume should always be written in a reverse chronological manner (i.e., the most recent job profile should come first).

> "Build your skills, Not your Resume."
> -Sheryl Sandberg

Curriculum Vitae (CV)

CV comes from a Latin word 'Curriculum Vitae' which means course of life. CV is more detailed than a resume as the latter contained only the brief summaries of job skills and experiences. CV on the other hand contains general educational qualifications, skills, degrees obtained and other professional affiliations of a candidate in a much more detailed manner.

Unlike a Resume which is more targeted and specific, a CV is mostly more general in nature and exhibits general expertise of a candidate. CV can go on till multiple pages too, if required. Usually, it is of 2-3 pages. CV is written in the usual chronological order unlike a resume.

CV vs Resume

Resume can be read quickly as it focusses on the key highlights of a prospective job candidate and hence is more suitable in private and industry-based firms. Resume is shorter in length and is more targeted and factual.

On the contrary, a CV is more detailed. It can be used in academic fields and positions which require a more thorough and detailed investigations into the candidature of a candidate.

Importance of CV/ Resume

- These are the only forms of professional communication in a business field and they create a lasting impression on the candidature of a person applying for a job.
- A well laid out Resume/ CV reflects competence, commitment and seriousness of a candidate.
- It allows organisations to effectively select the candidate as per their requirements. It makes the entire process fast.
- It describes the necessary skills, credentials and other accomplishments of a person in a brief and effective manner.
- A CV or a Resume is needed not just by graduates but also consultants, writers, academics etc.
- A nicely drafted Resume/ CV helps a person stand out in a crowd in a job market.

Together, a CV & Resume contains the following key points -

1. Personal Details (name, contact details, address, date of birth, nationality)
2. Educational Qualifications (from earliest to latest)
3. Work Profile/ Career History (name of company(s) worked with, nature of job, duration, achievements, internships, certifications, etc.)

4. Training and Skills achieved and developed (some skills can be social skills, practical skills, problem solving skills, technical skills, communication skills, creative skills etc.)

5. References (if any)

How to Write a CV?

• A key way of writing a good CV/ Resume is to invest some time in understanding one's own life and skills. Try to take some time out to know yourself better and how you can contribute and develop your own financial freedom through your life skills.

• One must think about possible areas in life they think they can work in.

• One must try to narrow down their area of interest and note down what interests them the most.

• Try to figure out which skills you possess.

• Make a list of things that you have done previously as part of any academic or extra-curricular activity.

• It must not be too lengthy or else it can be rejected and can even turn tiring for the employer or interviewer. It must not be too short also. An ideal length should be followed which gives all required information to the reader.

• It must be relevant to the organisation for which it is written for or else it might get rejected.

• A good CV must be organised neatly and must be presentable in all aspects. Layout should be good or else the reader might lose interest. The Resume/ CV must be visually appealing and neat.

• Make sure there are no typo errors or silly mistakes which will ruin the impression.

• A successful CV/ Resume is not just the one which is written, but also the one which is complimented equally by a good personality and presentation skills. In other words, in order to create a good impression, a candidate must be able to do justice to their CV/ Resume with adequate communication skills to justify their CV. Hence, a person should be as good as their CV indicates.

• You should know your CV well before appearing in an interview. A Resume/CV acts as a conversation breaker in an interview and will be the main point of focus for any interviewee. Most of the questions in an interview will be revolved only around a person's CV. Hence, a candidate must read their own CV thoroughly and must be prepared to answer anything related to it.

• Make sure to take reviews about your CV from job pundits and professionals whose positive feedback will help you gain confidence. It is a great way of self-improvement. You may also ask for feedback from your employer when you apply for a particular job.

---

4 Basics of a CV/ Resume

Therefore, a good Resume/CV must contain the following information about a person:

i. Who they are
ii. What skills they possess
iii. What they have done till now
iv. What they have achieved

These 4 basics should be present in every Resume/ CV. Every Resume/ CV must contain these basic details or else it will remain incomplete.

Practice

Q1. What are the major components of a CV?
Q2. What do you think is the single most important thing in a Resume?
Q3. What is the basic difference between CV & Resume?
Q4. What is Bio-Data? How is it different from CV/ Resume?

Let us now try to look at some examples of successful CVs/ Resume –

CURRICULUM VITAE

Dr. Akshi Pandita
501–B/2, Nehru Place
Delhi- 110019
880858580 (M)

<u>Profile</u>

Well qualified Graphic Designer with a Ph.D. in Graphic Designing. Experienced Head of the Creative team, a part of the core team of the Management and Promotion wing. Assistant Head Designer of annual campaigns. Committed to the job, good at meeting deadlines and has effective people skills.

<u>Key Skills and Achievements</u>

Typography: Excellent at making written words look visually attractive. Has the ability to turn basic designs into advanced and modern ones. Trained junior graphic designers in this most crucial skill of designing.

Coding: Experienced in working with advanced coding. Well experienced in working with Java and other advanced softwares. Developed software that comes handy for designers.

Branding: Created ideas and designs with the focus on the benefit of the company. Understands and serves the needs of the client for their desired results. Created logos for two international companies.

Creativity: Experienced at creating designs that stand out. Develops designs that fit the company's needs for a certain occasion or a campaign. Experienced at modifying designs as per the change in clients' requirements. Trained a team of 20 graphic designers and led a project with them that resulted in grand success.

Career Summary

2018-present: **SISD Advertising Company, Delhi**
Head Designer, Head of the Creative Team

2015-2018:   **Rossari Consultancy, Delhi**
Assistant Head Designer

2012-2015:   **IPCA Labs Pvt. Ltd., Dehradun**
Designer and Assistant Head of
Creative team

2011- 2012:   **Design & Visual Arts Training Institute, Dehradun**
Intern as a member of the Creative Team

Education and Training

- Ph.D. (Graphic Designing) from Indian Graphic University, Jammu & Kashmir
- Post-graduation in Visual Arts from Delhi College of Visual Arts, IP Extension, Delhi
- Graduation in BA (Hons) Journalism from University of Delhi, North Campus
- Diploma in Graphic Designing from NIFT, Delhi
- Advanced course in Graphic Designing and Coding, NIFT, Delhi

Personal Details

Date of Birth: 13th August 1989
Marital Status: Unmarried
Holds a driving license

Interests

Reading, basketball, running, sketching.

Here is another way of writing the same CV

<u>CURRICULUM VITAE</u>

Dr. Akshi Pandita
501–B/2, Nehru Place
Delhi- 110019
880859590 (M)

Profile
A well-qualified and experienced Graphic Designer & Ph.D. holder with great management and creative skills.

Work Experience

2018-present:	**SISD Advertising Company, Delhi** Head Designer, Head of the Creative Team
2015-2018:	**Rossari Consultancy, Delhi** Assistant Head Designer
2012-2015:	**IPCA Labs Pvt Ltd, Dehradun** Designer and Assistant Head of the Creative Team
2011-2012:	**Design and Visual Arts Training Institute, Dehradun** Intern as a member of the Creative Team

Educational Details

2014-2019:	Ph.D. (Graphic Designing) from Indian Graphic University, Jammu & Kashmir
2009- 2011:	Post Graduation in Visual Arts from Delhi College of Visual Arts, IP Extension, Delhi
2006- 2009:	Graduation in BA (Hons) Journalism from University of Delhi, North Campus
2005- 2006:	Passed 12th CBSE Board, Dehradun
2003- 2004:	Passed 10th CBSE Board, Dehradun

Training
2011: Advanced Course in Graphic Designing and Coding from NIFT, Delhi

2010: 6-months Diploma and Training in Graphic Designing from NIFT, Delhi

Personal Information

Status: Unmarried

Date of Birth: 13th August 1989

Likes

Running, Basketball, Reading and Sketching

Here is one more example of a CV –

Naina Dixit
202, Daulat Ram Lane
Civil Lines, Delhi-110007
(M) 886788889

Profile

An accomplished Trainer and Consultant with strong analytical and people skills and high experience of working in the field of Human Resources and Management. Led a team of 600 employees for a successful project. Contributed to Policy Making and Development projects showcasing great communication and management skills.

Key Accomplishments

* Trained 3 batches of interns who were later recruited by multinational companies.

* Led a project that included managing a team of 600 employees that resulted in 16% growth in the annual turnover of the company

* Organized a conference as the head of the management team on 'Human Resources: Vision of Future' at the national level.

Career History

<u>Rainbow Consultants</u> (2005-Present)

- Works with a team managing and overseeing the training services of multiple organizations and departments.
- Develops and designs courses and training programs.
- Manages projects and assists the management team.

<u>Nourish Foods Ltd.</u> (1998-2005)

- Promoted to the post of Assistant Manager.
- Managed human resources and recruitment process.
- Led a project that included managing a team of 600 employees that resulted in the 16% growth in the annual turnover of the company.

<u>LMC Insurance Services</u> (1995-1998)

- Worked in the Policy making department.
- Assisted and researched about the client's needs.
- Managed collaborations with the other companies.

Education

1992- 1995:   University of Delhi, M.Phil in History

1990- 1992:   University of Delhi, MA in History, Kirori Mal College

1987- 1990:   University of Delhi, BA in History, Hans Raj College

Training

2011-2012:   Attended training program at the National Human Resources Skill Development Seminar.

2005-2006:   Team Management course at the Birla Institute of HR Training.

Personal information

Marital status: Married

Date of Birth: 9th August 1980

Likes

Reading, Basketball and Sketching.

This type of CV is also known as a Targeted CV.

Practice

Q1. Imagine you have to write your CV for the job of your choice. By following the specimen example given in the study material, write a detailed CV for yourself by keeping in mind the points we have discussed above.

Q2. Prepare a covering letter for your CV which you have prepared in the previous question.

Given below are some more examples of successful CVs —

CURRICULUM VITAE
Tanishka Karotiya
B-789/22, East of Kailash
Delhi 110065
(M) 998666986

Profile

A Content Writer with high experience and great command over communication and analytics. Well qualified to develop content for multiple areas and fields. Trained and experienced in research and community work with strong people skills.

Key Accomplishments
Content Development and Research

Organized and contributed to the research programs for various organizations in the field of economic policy, social development campaigns and women empowerment programs.

Publishing

Published research articles and essays in *Cosmopolitan Journal of International Research Association*, ISSN 2244-6688. Published in the weekly column of *Daily Times Newspaper* called Unsung Voices, a peer reviewed column.

Creative Writing

Published a short story in the collection of short stories and poetry called "Our Voices, Our Rights" in *Journal of Ad Litteram*, ISSN 2499-9694, a peer-reviewed journal.

Social Media Manager

Managed social media handles of a company which resulted in increased social media engagement and gained new visitors and subscribers to the company's website and its newsletter.

Editing

Co-edited an anthology of a collection of fictional short stories and poems for children named "Summer Sings" for Khyati Publications.

Blogging

Runs a personal blog with over 1500 subscribers from different places across the world within 6 months of its beginning.

Career History

2019- Present:	**Khyati Publications, Delhi**
	Head Content Developer, Senior Editor & Researcher
2015- 2019:	**SMC Pvt. Ltd., Delhi**
	Co- editor, Reviewer and Senior Researcher
2011-2015:	**Marya Mahajan Musings, Delhi**
	Content writer and Junior Researcher
2010- 2011:	**Birla International Travels and Research Centre**
	Intern as a member of the Content Writing team

Education

- ◆ M.Phil in Journalism, University of Delhi, Delhi, 2015
- ◆ M.A. in Mass Communication, Delhi College of Arts, University of Delhi, Delhi, 2012

♦ B.A. in Mass Communication, Kirori Mal College, University of Delhi, Delhi, 2010

Training

♦ Attended training program at Mayur Publications for emerging writers and editors.
♦ Diploma in Creative Writing and Fiction Writing from Young Writers Association Research and Writing Institute and Training Centre.

Personal information

Date of Birth: 25th August 1993
Marital Status: Single
Holds a Driving license

Interests

Writing, trekking, social work & philanthropy.

Read the **comments** below to understand the dynamics of this CV in a more detailed and nuanced manner:

<u>Comments</u>

There is a lot of information in Tanishka's CV, still the CV is organized in a systematic way that takes less space and makes it easily readable. Font size and style should also get our attention.

This CV perfectly fits the work profile and career aspiration that Tanishka aims for, that is, writing. So, the details in the CV are centred around this to convey her potential as a content writer. Tanishka's interests talk about her personality and the things she is passionate about and her dedication for community service.

It is important to pay attention to the type of fonts you choose. Here important details are written in bold fonts that catch the attention of the readers. Hence, the CV is great to sell Tanishka's skills for the job. But it does not focus much on her qualities as a person.

Let us look at one final example of a CV –

Dr. Priyanka Mehta
38/C, Siddhartha Enclave
Lajpat Nagar
New Delhi – 110065

Profile

Highly qualified and experienced in the field of strategy making. Has great organizing and communication skills. Easily adaptive, handles pressure well. Self-motivated and motivates others as well. Aware of the current state and innovations in the strategy sector. Reliable as a leader and has great people skills.

Educational Details

- Ph.D. in Economics, University of Delhi, 2022
- M.Phil. in Economics, University of Delhi, 2018
- M.A. in Economics, Delhi College of Arts & Commerce, University of Delhi, 2014
- B.A. in Political Science, Kirori Mal College, University of Delhi, 2012.

Career Journey

- **2018 – Present:** SLC Consultant – Senior Strategist and Head of the Management Team. Researcher involved in conducting and evaluating research programs and Overseeing projects.
- **2016 – 2018:** Heidelberg Marketing – Assistant Manager. Worked in Marketing and Advertising Team. Contributed to the Development Cell and its Policy Making plans.
- **2014 – 2016:** Bharti Group of Communication Services. Assistant to the Management Head, Content Writer for the Marketing Unit.
- **2013 – 2014:** Indus Towers Telecommunication Services. Intern as a member of the Communication and Grievance Cell.

Interests

Likes to travel, paint, cook and spend time in nature.

Additional Information

Volunteer at Street Animals' Rescue NGO. Member of the New Voices Book Club. Holds a clean Driving License.

Dr. Priyanka Mehta
priyamehta@hotmail.com
(M) 0-971799717

Comments

Priyanka's aim is to get the position of a Strategist in a renowned marketing company. So significant emphasis is given on her educational background by introducing it first to show she is well qualified for the position with the required training and knowledge. Her personal information is given first in the CV, although it is not a decisive factor in her case. But the mention of a clean driving license will add on to her extra skills that can be seen as a factor of her mobility in case of traveling needed for the work.

Her profile shows her awareness of marketing policies and management sector that is reflective of her abilities that fit the job position she seeks. The mention of her abilities such as being "adaptive", "handling pressure" and being "self-motivated" are determinant of her suitability for the job role where these qualities are needed on a daily basis and they also stand for her ability to deal with people and handle stressful situations.

Priyanka's description of her work experience is well organized. The journey of a prospective employee's career is significant and of interest for every employer. She has systematically organized her career journey in a reverse chronological order which is the most preferred form by the majority of employers as it is easy to read and understand the growth of the aspirant over the years. It is important to understand it is always useful to mention every work experience that you have regardless of how huge or minor it is. Your work experience is a major factor that speaks for your abilities.

At the end, Priyanka has mentioned her interests and additional details that include her volunteering work and her involvement in creative activities outside her professional field. It is a great thing to include this as it speaks for her personhood and adds layers to her personality which are important factors for the employers to understand her attitude and personality. It also shows the additional skills that she possesses such as communication and organizing skills as a Member of the Book Club and her kind and concerning nature towards animals as a volunteer.

How to Write a Resume?

It can be safely assumed that the first and the most powerful impression that a job candidate can make on the interviewer is through a Resume. A good Resume allows an interviewer to quickly go through your credentials before seeing you in person. The proverb "First impression is the last impression" holds significant truth in this respect. As mentioned already, a Resume is less detailed in nature. A CV on the other hand is more detailed. A Resume is more or less a summary of a candidate's skills and is shorter than a CV.

Some points to be kept in mind while writing a Resume –

- Since a Resume is more targeted in its essence, hence it is advised to write in bullets.
- Also, since Resume is shorter than an average CV hence, we must be cautious in what to include and what to exclude from a Resume. Only key points should find a place in Resume.
- There is a need to prioritise as per our requirements in a Resume. Anything that is irrelevant or unimportant can be avoided in a Resume.

Things that a Resume should contain –

1. Contact Information (including name, phone number, address, business address, email, LinkedIn profile URL, etc).

2. A brief paragraph about what you have accomplished and your most important qualifications.

3. Areas of a candidate's core competences or core expertise should also be there.

4. Any trainings and certifications achieved should also be mentioned. Any other additional skills or professional associations, memberships etc. can also be included.

5. Do not include References in a Resume, unless asked for by the organisation to which you are applying to.

6. You may also use templates available on MS Word or any other popular resume building sites.

7. A regular font size of 12 can be used in writing a Resume. Avoid using multiple font styles. Use a maximum of 2 font styles like Calibri or Garamond style as they are easily readable.

Example of a Resume –

Alka K.
202 Civil Lines
Delhi-110007

Profile
A consultant with strong analytical and people skills and well experienced in the field.

Career History
2005-present: <u>Rainbow Consultants</u>
Working with a team managing and overseeing training services of multiple organizations. Develops and designs courses. Managing projects and assists management team.
1998-2005:   <u>Nourish Foods Ltd</u>
Promoted to the post of Assistant Manager. The job included to manage human resources and the recruitment process. Led a project that included managing a team of 600 employees that resulted in 16% increase in the annual turnover of the company.
1996-1998:   <u>LMC Insurance Services</u>
Worked in policy making department assisting and researching about clients' needs. Managed collaborations with other companies.

Education/ Qualification
1996-1998: Department of History, University of Delhi, M.Phil

---

1994-1996: Kirori Mal College, University of Delhi, MA in History

1991-1994: Hansraj College, University of Delhi, BA (Hons) in History

Training

2011-2012: Attended training programme at the National Human Resources Skill Development.

2005-2006: Team Management course at Birla institute of HR Training.

Personal Details

Status: Married
Date of Birth: 25th August 1974

Interests

Reading, basketball and sketching.

Bio-Data

The term 'Bio-data' means Biographical Data. As the nomenclature itself suggests, this usually contains biographical details of a person like date of birth, name, gender, marital status, nationality and other personal details. It also contains educational qualifications and other experiences and may on rare occasions also contain specific skills.

Bio-data is often used interchangeably with Resume and CV. But it is not correct. Bio-data has become more or less obsolete now in the contemporary business sphere and has been more correctly replaced with Resume and CV.

Practice

Q1. Why do we need CV/ Resume/ Bio-data?
Q2. What are the key differences between a CV and a Resume?
Q3. You are Aditi/Arjun. Write a CV to apply for the position of Sales Manager at a multinational company, mentioning your detailed education background, skills, work experience, etc.

Job Application Letter/ Covering Letter

Only creating a CV/ Resume or Bio-data is not enough. When we apply for a job, we need to supplement our CVs with a formal job-application letter as well.

Job-application letter can also be called as a covering letter. The need for a covering letter is equally important as it acts as a complement to your CV. It can further enhance your candidature. Whenever you are applying for a job, it must include a Covering Letter apart from your Resume. It is important to note that a job-application letter is not a replacement of a CV. It will only add to the overall impression of your job application.

Importance of Job-Application Letter/ Covering Letter –

- It creates a more professional impact on your CV/ Resume. It makes your application more business-like.
- It shows that you are keen for the job and you have taken an extra step of interest. It will hence create a great first impression.

Job-Application Letter – How to Write One?

- Keep your letter short and within one page. It should not exceed one A4 sized sheet.
- You may write a hand-written covering letter to add more personal touch to your application. In case your writing is not very neat, you may type it out too.
- Your covering letter is a great chance for you to sell your skills in front of an employer by showcasing key points relevant to the employer. It must arouse interest from the employer.
- A good job-application letter must also act as a brief introduction to your CV/ Resume.

- The letter should not be a mere repetition but only as an introduction to your accompanying Resume/ CV. Do not repeat things or it will look redundant and repetitive.
- Be cordial in approach and tone while writing a covering letter and always end on a polite note.
- A job-application letter or covering letter is like any other formal letter and hence the format for it remains more or less similar to what we have in a formal letter

---

Practice

Q1. Why is a Job-Application Letter needed along with CV/Resume?

Q2. What are the key benefits of a Job-Application Letter?

Q3. You have to apply for a job of a Senior Executive Administrator at Honda Cars Pvt Ltd. You are currently working as Deputy Executive Administrator at Toyota Cars Pvt Ltd. Write a Job-Application letter for the same introducing your candidature to the employer.

Note- Do not write a CV. Only a Job-Application letter.

Mr. Himanshu Bidi is a Dy. Sales Manager at Infosys Ltd. He now wants to apply for the post of a Sr. Sales Manager at Wipro Ltd. Let us try to look at the format and example of a Job application letter in this case –

Himanshu Bidi
Wipro Limited
Sarjapur Road, Bengaluru – 786599

Subject: Job-application letter for Senior Sales Manager at Wipro Ltd.

Respected Sir/ Ma'am,

I am interested in applying to your firm for the post of Senior Sales Manager as per your requirement. I am enclosing my CV in connection with this.

I am currently working at Infosys Ltd. as Deputy Sales Manager and carry a decade long experience in the same. I am adept at public dealings with plenty of enthusiasm. I am comfortable with flexible working hours and I believe I possess the required skills for this post.

I would request you to have a look at my CV. Looking forward to seeing you to discuss more on this position in detail.
Himanshu Bidi
Deputy Sales Manager
Infosys Ltd
Noida, Uttar Pradesh

Look at the comments below to understand the dynamics of writing a job-application letter in a more nuanced manner.

Comments

The above letter has a neat detailed layout and the candidate, Mr. Bidi has shown his interest in the position. The letter also gives a brief outline of his previous job experience. This job application letter acts as an introduction to the candidature of Ravi and also manages to create a professional first impression for his employer.

Notice that the letter is brief and short in length. It is just a general introduction of the candidate and not a detailed explanation of his CV. The CV should be attached separately.

Documentation

Documentation or Documenting involves the process of noting down any event, procedure, proceedings for business purposes. It can also be used to give details about any object/ project/ event, etc. Documentation process also involves collecting, storing, retrieving, and sharing data in an organisation. Documentation is hence a part of routine business transactions within professional spheres.

Documentation is basically a part of core business communications. Every organisation has its own aspects, functions ranging from internal correspondences, administrative correspondences to meetings and preparation of reports and proposals. For these purposes a proper documenting is required. Hence, the art of documenting can be useful inside a business organisation in properly organising information related to its various aspects.

Importance of Documentation

- Documentation can be used to provide targeted and useful information in an organisation aimed at a targeted audience.
- Documentation helps in achieving uniformity and standardisation in an organisation.
- Documenting can also be useful in preparation of annual reports of a company.
- It can also be used in data management and collation.
- Documentation can be used alongside charts, diagrams, figures, and facts to ease out the management of data.

Document – How to Write One?

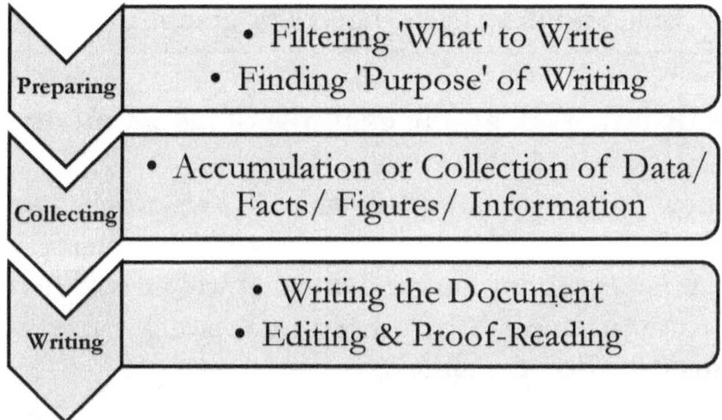

1ˢᵗ step is Preparing – This includes making preliminary preparations about what to write. You need to filter the information that you will put in the document. You need to understand the purpose of writing this document and also try to figure out the audience you are writing for.

2ⁿᵈ step is Collecting – This step includes jotting down all points, and collecting all information to be written in the document. This step includes collecting the data that would be written in the document.

3rd step is Writing – This step involves outlining and organising the document. All editing and formatting can be done in this step only. This is where the actual writing of the document occurs.

The flow-chart given below will help in understanding the 3 steps required to write a document efficiently:

---

4 Basics of a Document

1. A good document is a product of proper planning, research, and collection of data.
2. One needs to be aware of the technical terms in any organisation to create a dynamic documentation.
3. Documentation includes facts and hence it must be authentic and credible.
4. Documentation does not only mean writing paragraphs of information. It is always better to use visual aids, bullet points, charts, figures or graphs in a document.

Let us now look at one example of a document:

A new garments company named *Kriyansh Fabrics* has been established recently. Prepare a profile of this company in the form of a document mentioning the items that will be sold here as well as price of the products. Any other promotional offers, schemes or discounts can also be included.

Kriyansh Fabrics PVT LTD
Mukherjee Nagar, Delhi- 110007

About Us:

Kriyansh Fabrics is a newly founded company that manufactures clothes and quality apparels for our customers. Our company's founder is Mr. Karan Singh who began his journey in this industry as a part time worker in a clothes showroom during his college days. His close and early experience in the industry ignited in him a passion to cater to the need of sustainable fashion.

Kriyansh Fabrics is dedicated to provide services to this industry and create a mark on the same through our quality maintenance and customer satisfaction. In today's world where everything is driven by 'trend' and 'fashion', *Kriyansh Fabrics* promises the best quality products to keep you up to date at a budget friendly price.

Products:

- ❖ Ethnic Wear (men/ women/ kids)
- ❖ Formal Wear
- ❖ Sarees
- ❖ Suits and Kurtas
- ❖ Men's Fashion (shirts/ T-shirts/ pants/ jeans)
- ❖ Women's Western Wear
- ❖ Kids Fashion

Our readymade products come in different types of categories based on the type of cloth and material.

Introductory offers:

- ❖ 40% off on your first purchase
- ❖ Buy 3 get 1 free on shirts
- ❖ 1 gift card on every purchase above 800₹

Price range:

We have kept our prices affordable to cater to the widest audience possible. The price range of each product varies, starting from 400₹ and goes till 4200₹.

Tips for care/ maintenance:

- ❖ Always wash with cold water
- ❖ Never use hot water
- ❖ Iron clothes at low setting to increase their shelf life
- ❖ To maintain the shine and quality of silk products

always dry clean and avoid harsh detergents
- ❖ Avoid washing clothes excessively to keep their natural shine and quality intact

Facilities:

- ❖ We offer the facility to rent clothes as well
- ❖ We deal in raw material as well – all types of fabrics are available, like Cotton Blend, Cotton Modal, Cotton Georgette (With & Without Lining), Viscose, Polyester, Silk Blend, Linen, Denim, Chiffon, Satin, Velvet, Wool, etc
- ❖ Exchange of product is available within 2 days of purchase
- ❖ We offer customization options as well
- ❖ Best quality and trendy products at a very reasonable price

Customer outreach and services:
Our customer care helpline numbers are:
011-5656907 (Off)
0-799395990 (Mob)
WhatsApp helpline:
+91-674947404

Customer care services are open Monday to Friday from 9:00 am to 8:00 pm; on Saturday from 10:00 am to 6:00 pm.
Webpage – www.kriyansh9fashions.co.in.tech
Facebook – @kriyanshfashions9official
Instagram – @kriyanshfashions9fabrics

Timings of the shop:
Monday to Friday- 8:00 am to 10:00 pm
Saturday- 8:00 am to 1:00 pm
#Note: Sunday Closed.

Address:
C-301, Block C, GTB Nagar Market, Delhi – 110007. Near Malka Ganj Metro Station.

Practice

Q1. What is the meaning of Documentation?

Q2. What are the steps to prepare a Document?

Q3. You are going to start a publication house named *Kalamos Literary Publishers*. Prepare a documentation example for the same mentioning the details of the types of books, team of your editors, publication charges and process along with early bird offers to your writers and other customers.

Advertisements and Invitations

Advertisements

In the current world, advertisement is of prime importance when it comes to business and professional life. The job-oriented world thrives on marketing through advertisement. No advertisement means no growth. Advertisements at the same hand is a very important and responsible sphere with multiple ethical responsibilities.

Advertisement is not just about creating an ad, but also about finding the right audience, customers, preparing marketing strategy and creating responsible advertisements. Nowadays, job advertisement is a basic tool used by almost all companies to increase their footprint and to invite talented workforce to their company. In the private sector creating an advertisement hence has become a necessity and a basic job skill.

The simple purpose of an advertisement is to make people buy a product or a service. To create a successful ad, you need to find relevant material. This can be done by doing adequate market research. You have to catch the audience's attention while drafting an advertisement.

How to write Advertisements?

- The first step to create a good advertisement is to first find your target audience. This is extremely crucial.
- Then create a message which needs to be circulated in the advertisement for that targeted audience.

- You must determine and understand the response of the target audience for your advertisement to be successful.

- You have to market your advertisement in a manner which shows the viewers the advantages of using the product/ services.

- Advertisement campaigns do not end with creation of advertisements. It goes beyond that by also assessing the impact it creates on the respondents. This response mapping is also a crucial form of advertisement campaigns.

- Ads must be logical for the general public, or else they will not be interested in endorsing it.

- The headline, or the title is of supreme importance in any advertisement. Many people do not read the whole advertisement if the title is not engaging enough. So, create a catchy title. Only an interesting title can engage an audience to read the whole advertisement.

- The title should have a wide appeal and must connect with the readers.

- Ads should always be positive and transformative in nature. It must come as a novelty in the job sphere.

- You may use diagrams, images, graphs, pie-charts, witty one-liners to create a different advertisement which attracts people's attention. This is because a good advertisement is seen first and read later. To make your audience see it you have to add some eye-catchy ideas.

- Always use multiple and diverse channels to market your ads. Social media again can play a very important role in this.

- Advertisements should touch your audience. They should be able to relate to the product. Hence, try to find points of common contact and mention them in the ad.

- Many a times, ads contain general things which are vague. Stick to specific and concrete details about the product you are trying to sell.

- Emphatic and power words should always be added in an advertisement. These words attract attention to the ad. Use words such as mastery, exclusive, special, bargain, brand new, profit, exciting, etc.

- Start your ad with a pertinent question, which will make people answer it.
- Paragraphs should be short in length and not vague.
- Use a readable font which is easy to read by the audience.
- Make sure to declutter the space. There is no need to fill all spaces in the ad. There should be no information overload. Some blank space should be there to make the ad breathable.

> "Many a small thing has been made large by the right kind of advertising."
> **-Mark Twain**

Given below is an example of an advertisement by a company called *International Communications* who is looking for a candidate for their company as a graphic designer. It is an example of a job-advert.

International Communications

We HELP you CONNECT

Looking 4 Graphic Designers

Here is an opportunity you would not like to miss to join a constantly growing multi-national company. *International Communications* is the most trusted and leading company in the emerging field of telecommunications.

Looking for talented and dynamic artists to join us!

Responsibilities:
- Designing illustrations for the company's campaigns
- Developing concepts and ideas and assisting the creative team
- Planning ideas and designing advertisements

Pre-requisites:
- Experience in graphic designing

> • Knowledge of designing software and other designing tools like Canva
>
> • Team working skills
>
> **Our company offers weekly off on Saturdays and Sundays with a handsome salary and a learning experience with many other opportunities.**
>
> **International Communications**
> **24, Lawrence Road, New Delhi - 67**
> job_apply@ic.in.co

> "Advertising is the greatest art form of the 20th century."
> -Marshall McLuhan

Invitations

Invitation can be of any type. In business correspondences, the range of invitation varies widely. Some invitations which can be written are —

- Formal invitations
- E-mail invitations
- Invitation to an interview
- Invitation to speaker at a conference
- Invitation for some special function
- Reply accepting invitation
- Reply declining invitation

Usually, an invitation contains the following heads –

i.   Recipient's name or the person(s) who is/ are being invited
ii. Name and address of the person who is extending the invitation
iii. Date
iv. Time

v.   Venue

vi.   Brief description of the event for which the invite is being sent

Example of Invitation

<table>
<tr><td>

The Literary Society (Lit-Soc)
Hansraj College, University of Delhi
is delighted to invite
Prof. (Dr) T.K. Karotiya
as
Chief Guest
at the
10th Annual Foundation Day Celebrations
of
The Literary Society
at 9:00 AM on Saturday 24th July 2025
The Council, Literary Society (Lit-Soc)
Hansraj College, University of Delhi
North Campus
Delhi-110007
RSVP by 24th July 2025

</td></tr>
</table>

Note – The format for an email invitation however differs from the regular invitations. Everything remains the same but the formatting is changed. Use formal sentences like "our company seeks your auspicious presence", "request your presence", "solicit your appearance on the event", etc. while writing a formal invitation.

Example of email invitation –

Dear Hrithika,

I am Tannu, Student Council President of Delhi College of Arts & Commerce (DCAC), University of Delhi. It gives me immense pleasure to inform you that to continue our everlasting journey of togetherness, DCAC is going to organize its 31st Annual Alumni Meeting on 9th May 2025. There will be many cultural performances by the college music and theater groups, food stalls and interesting games.

As a former student of the college, you are invited to attend the 31st Annual Alumni Meeting. Please come to spend a day with us and recall the fond memories of your college life along with your fellow batchmates. I request you to stay for lunch as well after the cultural programs.

Please find the entry pass in the attachment. We will be delighted to have you with us. Waiting for your graceful and positive response!

Best wishes

Tannu
Student Council President
DCAC, University of Delhi
Netaji Nagar, New Delhi – 110023

While writing an e-mail invitation you can use a few pictographical entries, or broad headings. But keep it to a minimal. A few would do.

Example of an invitation sent through a letter (inviting speaker to a seminar) –

The Delhi Institute of Theatre and Visual Arts
22nd Nov' 2025

Prof. T.K. Karotiya
10, Civil Lines, New Delhi

Dear Prof. Karotiya,

Greetings!

Our Department will be organizing a seminar at The Delhi Institute of Theatre and Visual Arts, Delhi on 22nd November 2025 with the theme *'Modern Indian Theatre in 21st Century: Theatrical Innovations and Scopes'*. Around 100-120 participants are expected to attend the seminar, comprising of theatre artists, actors, directors, scholars and faculty members.

As a domain expert and an authority on contemporary Indian theatre, I on behalf of our Department will request your august presence to deliver a speech on the aforementioned subject on 22nd November 2025, 10:00 AM onwards. We would cover your travel expenses, lodging expenses and would also like to provide an honorarium to you for your scholarly lecture.

I have enclosed the detailed draft of the programme along with this letter. We are hopeful that you would be able to accept our invitation. Meanwhile we would be glad to know if we can arrange any equipment for you.

I look forward to your response.

Yours sincerely

PR Department
The Delhi Institute of Theatre and Visual Arts
Mandi House, Copernicus Marg
New Delhi-110260

Practice

Q1. As the head of your company's PR team, create an invitation to invite Dr. Saumya Sagar, a senior editor of Khyati Publications as the chief guest of your company's 20th Founders Day celebration.

Q2. What are the key ways to draw attention to an advertisement?

Q3. How many types of invitations are there? Explain each of them.

Q4. How is an email invitation different from an invitation letter? Explain the differences between these two types of invitations.

Q5. What does an invitation consist of? Write down its major components.

Poster Designing – Canva

Canva is a platform for graphic designing. It was founded in Australia in 2013. This is mostly used for creating posts for social media. It is useful for making presentations visually better and to create other visuals and graphics. Anyone can use this platform for free and if you want to use its advanced services you can subscribe to its paid versions like Canva Pro. There is another advanced version of it known as Canva for Enterprises. Canva also prints and ships products.

Canva is one of the most advanced quality and useful tool for graphic designing and for creating many other types of visual content. It is very useful for educational purposes as well. It can be used to work on projects and it is useful for educators and students to learn graphic designing. It is a free tool which makes it easy to access for students and teachers as well. It provides multiple free templates for every purpose. It is a great platform for photo editing as well. It is easily accessible as you can download it on any device and it is popular for its user-friendly nature.

Practice

Q1. What is the significance of designing a poster in professional life?

Q2. How is Canva a suitable tool for poster designing?

Negotiations

Negotiation is the interaction including at least two parties cooperating to show up at a commonly satisfactory goal of at least one issue. It is a compromise bartering process which, when led well, leaves all parties fulfilled about the outcome and focused on accomplishing it. The main target of a discussion is to arrive at an answer of the contention to the common fulfilment and advantage of all the negotiating parties.

Negotiations can happen both in formal and casual circumstances. Formal discussions occur to resolve labor disputes, union strikes or requests of laborers. In a casual/informal situation meeting between individuals is never decided ahead of time.

Process of Negotiation

Negotiation is a complex process that goes through several stages before reaching the desired outcome. Most researchers agree that the negotiating process has four broad stages. They are called:

- opening a negotiation
- exchange of information
- change of position
- closing

In the **first stage**, one is socializing, forming relationships and making new acquaintances. They aid in the establishment of a foundation or in future negotiations. In these meetings, one should try to analyze the other side and form a social relationship.

In the **second stage**, information is exchanged and expectations of the issue to be negotiated are placed on the table in front of both parties. Each party's strength is determined by its needs, resources, and ability to negotiate.

The concerned parties attempt to negotiate issues to their advantage in the **third stage**. Each side attempts to persuade the other to accept its point of view and to make compromises on its position to the benefit of the other.

In the **final stage**, the parties attempt to bargain over issues to their advantage. Both parties try to get the best possible deal.

> "Let us never negotiate out of fear. But let us never fear to negotiate."
> -John F. Kennedy

Effective Negotiation

To achieve the best result, there are two types of negotiating strategies: cooperative and competitive. It is always best to use a combination of the two whenever possible.

Following are some of the strategies for effective negotiation:

- Maintain a positive and non-aggressive demeanor at the negotiating table.
- Try to persuade and convince the opposing party of the benefits of accepting your proposal.
- It is important to express your point of view, but it is also critical to listen to the opposing viewpoint.
- Do not interrupt or comment during the other side's presentation. Interruptions not only disrupt the flow but can also irritate the other party.
- Maintain a corporate and optimistic atmosphere, and if you wish to ask a question, use a calm tone rather than an aggressive or hostile one.
- If there is a stalemate or a heated argument, take a brief break. This not only calms both parties but also allows them to re-examine the proposals and reconsider their bargaining position.
- Personal preferences or egos should never be allowed to influence the bargaining process; all challenges are more essential than individuals or personalities.
- Summarize the discussion to avoid future confusions or miscommunication.

- The summary should be in writing so that no one can revise it later.

- Include a legal clause if required to make sure that there is no scope for going back on previously negotiated concerns.

- A negotiation is a type of agreement for both parties. This must be kept in mind while attempting to negotiate.

- Always be ready to gain some and lose some in a negotiation process. So, it is important to prioritize your needs. Try not to make concessions on crucial matters whilst giving up on minor ones.

- You should be clear about the goals you would like to achieve; it will help you focus better during the bargaining process.

- The decision made in the end should be regarded as final. After that, there should be no changes.

> "Information is a negotiator's greatest weapon."
> -Victor Kiam

Practice
Q1. What are the different stages in the process of successful negotiations?

Interview

Interview – Promotion Interview, Job Interview, Business Interview

As the term itself suggests, an interview means viewing each other. It is akin to two people viewing each other. The types of interview may range from job interviews, personal interviews, celebrity interviews, to interviews of politicians, online interviews etc.

In this module we will look at professional and business interviews. This is an essential form of professional communication as everyone at some point of time has to face an interview. It is a prerequisite for any job and cannot be done away with. Interviews are conducted with an aim to understand a candidate's potential, competence, and their skills in the job for which they are applying. Interviews are essential not only at the level of job recruitment but also at the level of counselling, promotion, delegation of duties and other responsibilities.

Interview usually consists of an interviewee, the person who is being interviewed. And the person who asks questions is known as an interviewer. Often, there is a panel of 2 or more members who conduct an interview of a candidate. Sometimes, the number of members in the panel can go up to 7 to 8 also. Interview is basically a form of oral professional communication. It is also a sort of negotiation between the interviewer and the interviewee.

The focus of this part of the book fwill be on professional interviews. Professional interviews as an umbrella term will be used here to include job interviews, recruitment interviews, promotion interviews and business interviews. These types of interviews are conducted in a question-answer format where the nature of the interview remains formal.

> "I hate interviews - but you have to do them."
> -Jackie Chan

How to prepare for an Interview?

Before appearing for an interview, a prospective job candidate should prepare for the interview. Appearing for an interview without preparation is simply unprofessional and also lowers the chances of selection considerably. Some ways in which a candidate can prepare for an interview are –

- Make a list of all of your achievements and experiences so that you may be able to answer swiftly when asked about it.
- Prepare a comprehensive CV by putting all your detailed information, experience, and all other relevant information in it. It should be a comprehensive CV and must be visually appealing. Follow all steps required for the preparation of a professional CV.

- Only preparing a detailed CV is not sufficient. What is perhaps even more significant is to know your CV thoroughly. Many candidates do not revise their CV which puts them in an uncomfortable position in front of the interviewer. Your CV is the only piece of written information in front of your employer and hence you must be thoroughly attuned with the information in your CV.

- Be presentable in the interview. It creates a pleasant impression on the interviewer. Shabby dresses should be avoided and a formal outlook should be presented in front of the interview panel.

- Always listen to the question completely before answering. One should always be a good listener to succeed in an interview. Sometimes the interviewee responds before the question is completed. This leaves a bad impression and you may come across as an impatient candidate. This may make you look highly unprofessional.

- Try to answer the questions in a brief manner. The longer your answer, the more disinterested the panel members become. Be specific and answer with brevity in a concise manner. For this you need to practice.

- Never try to answer what you do not know. It is always better to admit it and apologise politely instead of bluffing the interviewer. One should politely deny the question to which one does not have the answer to.

- Body language should always be positive. Watch videos on the internet to learn the art of persuasive speaking and confident body language. Watching mock interviews can help a candidate gain some confidence to sit in an interview. Also, reading self-help books on body language goes a long way in preparing a candidate for a job interview.

- Do a personal SWOT analysis. SWOT is an acronym for 'Strength, Weakness, Opportunity, Threat.' Conducting your own SWOT analysis makes you aware of your strengths and weaknesses and makes you more confident about sitting in an interview. Make a list of these and keep them handy for any question.

- You must sound enthusiastic and in high spirits. Do not sound dull or bored as it decreases the chances of selection.

- Always prepare a two-minute introduction about yourself in advance. This is because many interviewers ask you to introduce yourself to the panel members. While answering such questions, always remember to keep your answer limited to business matters. Keep the answer business related or related to the job in question.

- Nothing can beat the homework for an interview. Homework means preparing in advance for the possible questions that can be asked in an interview. Always do a background check of the organisation or institute you are applying at. Gather information about the employing agency from the internet, newspapers, and existing working employees of the organisation. An interviewer will always give favourable marks to a candidate who shows interest in the workplace and organisation.

- Nowadays with the advent of digital communication post covid pandemic, many organisations conduct interviews in the online mode as well. Preparation for this kind of an interview is slightly different than a regular face-to-face interview but overall, the essence remains the same.

- The purpose of any interview is to hire the right candidate for a job. The interviewer would like to select a person who understands the working environment of the organisation. Hence, it is always better to research in detail about the job profile for which you are appearing for the interview. Also, research about the organisation and its environment.

- At times it is beneficial to anticipate the questions that might be asked in the interview. Make a list of those questions and prepare answers for them.

- You can appear for mock interviews conducted by various personality development firms. They will also provide constructive criticism to your interview.

- Always carry all your credentials, testimonials, certificates in a file and if possible, keep multiple photocopies for the same.

- Never use slang language or behave overtly casual in front of the interview panel. Your language should be straightforward and positive. It should be neither too formal nor too casual.

Online Interviews

As we know, ever since the pandemic there has been a huge increase in digital communication and it has become a new normal now. A lot of organizations are now conducting online interviews via Skype, G-Meet & MS Teams. Online interviews have to be dealt with differently than a face-to-face interview.

Some points to be kept in mind while giving online interviews:

- Keep your username official. A casual username on your video conferencing ID will create a poor impression on the interviewer.
- Your profile picture should be formal and official in such an interview.
- Conduct a thorough functionality test of the internet, camera, and microphone before preparing for an online interview. There should be no mechanical barriers to your communication.
- You should always keep your video switched on. Wear appropriate official dress and select your background wisely. You would not want your interviewer to see a cluttered background. Always go for a neat background.

Example of an Interview –

You are a journalist working with The Hindustan Times who has been assigned the task of interviewing Miss. Ashka, a teacher in a remote village of India who has dedicated her life towards bringing a change in the rural education scenario. You have to conduct this interview to know about her experience and challenges of teaching in a village. Write an interview with her based on this theme.

Interview of Ms. Ashka

Journalist: Good morning, Ms. Ashka. We are pleased to have you among us today. You won the Global Teacher's Prize at such a young age and you have been working for the betterment of rural education since long. You are the best person to tell us what are the challenges of teaching in a village.

Ashka: Thanks for having me for this interview. It is a pleasure to be here. The challenges that we face while teaching in a village needs to be highlighted to the society and the government. I hope today I would be able to highlight the challenges of teaching in a rural environment and I would love to share how I overcame some of the obstacles myself.

Journalist: Miss Ashka, can you tell us about the ruling cause that hinders education in villages?

Ashka: In our school, children from nearby villages come and attend the classes. The major problem which they face is mode of transportation. Firstly, they are required to travel large distances by foot and the roads are not proper. Moreover, many times children may have to cross rivers, fields and forests. Many children say these routes are not safe and specially for girls. This causes high dropout rates. Mid-day-meal schemes are irregular because of which children remain hungry and eventually drop out of the school. Even parents are unwilling to send their child to school. Parents engage their child in household chores and field work. There is also a lack of motivation in students.

Journalist: Are the village girls allowed to attend schools?

Ashka: The idea of girl education is not very popular here. Rarely girls come to schools. Girls are expected to stay at home and perform household chores.

Journalist: This is quite alarming! It is also seen that schools in villages have poor infrastructure. How does this cause obstacles in your way of teaching? How would you describe the infrastructure of the school?

Ashka: Village schools are different from city schools. The infrastructure here is not good. There are no classrooms, no proper roofs, and no benches. Even water and electricity are not available. It becomes difficult to teach in an environment like this where facilities are very less.

Journalist: Then how did you manage to overcome these problems?

Ashka: I overcame these challenges by bringing puzzles, charts, toys and books, so that this could be of some help. Moreover, I encourage my students to make something or the other innovative, so that they could have maximum exposure to application-based knowledge. Last year from our school a student named Bina constructed a small robot from household scrap, leaves and branches. She also received an award for the same.

Journalist: That is brilliant! So, this really keeps up the interest of the student?

Ashka: This is not always the case. Studying without electricity and internet becomes monotonous, and this results in lack of motivation. Therefore, they require a constant motivating force for studying or else most of them prefer to choose household chores and farm work rather than studying in school.

Journalist: As a teacher, what are the problems that you face in teaching these children?

Ashka: As the villages are secluded from cities, it is a long distance for us to teach in these schools. There are hardly any schools here and jobs are very few. The wages that we get is very less and due to all these reasons, not many teachers come here to teach. The teaching staff is very small.

Journalist: How do you think that these problems can be handled so these children can have a bright future ahead?

Ashka: The government should look into this matter and provide the necessary resources and infrastructure. Providing regular mid-day-meals would also encourage students to come to school. Spreading awareness about girl's education will be helpful for the future. Because today's young generation will become tomorrow's future and it is important to educate all, leaving none behind.

Journalist: You are doing a great service for the nation and for the society in general. We hope more people like you contribute to this cause; you are a source of hope and inspiration for many. Is there anything else that you would like to add?

Ashka: Every child has the right to study and do wonder. This right should not be robbed off because of poor infrastructure, internet connection, electricity and lack of transportation. It is the duty of the educated ones to spread their wonders of knowledge. I hope the government will look upon this and provide the necessary facilities. Till then we can try our best to make these children understand the importance of education. Thank you for having me and highlighting my work.

Journalist: Thank you, Miss Ashka. Your words are really inspiring. We wish you good luck for your future and for the cause that you are working for. Thank you once again!

Ashka: You're welcome!

> "Don't underestimate the power of the nonverbal. You'd be amazed how many people come in for interviews with poor posture, weak handshakes, and blank stares."
> -Nicole Williams

Job Interview

Let us now look at an example for a job interview. This is a job interview between Rida, a candidate for the position of Head Content Developer in a company and the recruiter of the company.

Interviewer: Good morning, Miss Rida! Welcome to SMC International. I am Kavya, I am the manager of the Marketing department and a member of the recruitment panel.

Rida: Good morning, ma'am! It is nice to meet you.

Interviewer: Nice to meet you too! How are you doing nowadays?

Rida: I am doing well, ma'am. How about you?

Interviewer: I am doing well too. Thanks! Now we shall begin with your interview, shall we?

Rida: Yes, ma'am! We shall.

Interviewer: So, Miss Rida, we have a vacant position for the head of our content developing team. Our company is one of the few leading companies that provide services in multiple fields as per the needs of our clients. And you are here to apply for the position of Head Content Developer of our company.

Rida: Yes ma'am, you are right. As a content developer with the experience of more than 8 years, I believe I will be able to do the justice with this position.

Interviewer: Yes, Rida. We like your confident approach to it. So, tell us something about yourself and how you are a suitable match for this position.

Rida: I thrive when I write. Words have always been my forte and I enjoy writing and dealing with content on a large variety of topics and utilize my skills for the best result for my company. Apart from writing content as a freelancer for 12 years, I have led a team of 8 content writers in *Saransh Consultancy* for 5 years. I have been a trainer at the same company's internship program and I have trained 2 batches of interns too, consisting of more than 15 interns in each batch for content writing.

Interviewer: That is really impressive, Rida! So, tell us what sets you apart from other content developers? What is your USP?

Rida: Thank you for this question. I would say my USP is my communication skills. I have always been excellent when it comes to communication. It always worked as a great benefit when I dealt with customers and clients. All the employers in the past have praised me for being empathetic. My listening skills allow me to be persistent when it comes to solving issues for my clients and working as per their demands. I believe these are the skills that are most useful to understand and serve the needs of the clients.

Interviewer: That's right! I agree with your answer. So, what types of strategies would you use to get new clients?

Rida: The process of getting new clients is a very competitive one. A lot of times I have talked to potential clients who were looking for content developers and writers who best serve their needs and fit their budget as well. So, prior to discussions with any client, I would make sure to do my research on the content writing services they are using at the moment. If our content agency provides better and more financially accessible services, I would be focused to convey this to them. My focus would also be on asking them the things that they like and dislike about the current service provider they have hired and try to explain how our company is the most suitable one to serve their expectations and needs.

Apart from this, I would also propose a consultation session for free to our potential client. Prior to this consultation session, I would have a meeting with the content development department and the marketing unit to understand the client's requirements, locate them on the basis of our services and explore and research to meet their needs. At the end, I would make the offer and show our client the plan for their requirements along with a budget that suits them and an easy payment method.

Interviewer: This is excellent! Among all these things, keeping up with the deadlines is one of the most important qualities that we are looking for in our candidates. So, tell me about your idea and strategies to manage deadlines.

Rida: I understand why this is a major concern for employees. Meeting the deadlines is one of the foundational steps towards building the reputation of the company and long-term partnerships with the clients and maintaining it as well. To keep up with the deadlines, my strategy is to plan ahead in advance and break the task into chunks so it becomes easy to assign these tasks to the other members of the team according to their expertise. Apart from this, time management, strategically planning and coordinating with the team are the most important factors to keep up with the deadlines without compromising with the quality of our work.

Interviewer: Perfect, Rida! I am really happy with your comprehensive answers. I admire your confidence in your skills and experience that speaks through your answers. Your interview is done. I request you to kindly wait for the results of the interview that would be released in a couple of days. Till then take care. Have a great day ahead!

Rida: Thank you so much, ma'am for your kind words. I am looking forward to hearing from you. Thank you and good day!

<u>**Comments**</u>

The questions asked by interviewer are mostly common and broad but the answers by Rida are focused and central to the job position she is seeking. An interviewee's answers must always be targeted and focused without digressing from the question asked. Her answers revolve around the job role and she keeps them to the point without beating around the bush.

You will notice that Rida never left a chance to talk about her experience. It is important to let your employee know that you are well experienced and have dealt with the tricky situations in the past, or you are prepared enough to handle future job assignments. This adds value to your candidature and you stand a great chance of bagging the job.

Interview – Say This Instead of That

There are several clichéd words and phrases that we often use in an interview. These phrases are used by the majority of candidates while giving any interview and thereby this reduces the benefit one can get out of it. Interview boards are almost always looking for something different in any prospective candidate. This is where a candidate needs to stand out and use phrases which do not sound redundant.

Some of the ways in which an interviewee can use better phrases are mentioned below. In the form of a table several instances are shown and alongside are shown better responses which will make your vocabulary stand out and will surely leave a lasting impression in the minds of the interviewers.

Instead of That	**Say This**
I'm hardworking	I consistently go above and beyond in my tasks
I'm result oriented	I regularly achieve my performance targets
I'm a problem solver	I enjoy tackling complex challenges & finding solutions
I'm detail oriented	I have a keen eye for catching errors
I'm passionate about my work	I am deeply devoted to achieving excellence in my field
I'm a quick learner	I adapt swiftly to new tools & technologies
I'm flexible	I adapt easily to dynamic circumstances & challenges
I'm motivated	I am self-driven & consistently strive for excellence
I'm a good communicator	I excel at articulating ideas clearly and concisely

Comments

In each of the instance mentioned above, you will realise that there is a better version available. The readers will notice that the phrases used sound more professional and are also more explanatory in nature.

The phrase "I am self-driven & consistently strive for excellence" is much better than the bland "I'm motivated". The latter sounds too clichéd and drab. Being motivated means being self-driven while at the same time strive consistently for excellence. The former phrase explains the idea in a much more professional and sophisticated manner. All of it leaves a lasting impression on the interview panel and increases the chances of scoring good marks in any interview.

It is also interesting to note that these phrases above can also be used in building your CV/ Resume, though it should be done in moderation and only sparingly.

Practice

Q1. What do you understand by interview? Explain its significance in professional life.

Q2. What are the key steps to prepare and qualify for an interview?

Q3. You are Tara/Tarun, prepare an example of an interview for a job of your choice.

Public Relations (PR)

PR (Public Relations) alludes to the essential correspondence from an organisation to the general population to keep up with, or develop the public image of an organisation. Corporate organisations depend a lot on their image in the public. The future growth perspectives of any business firm depend a lot on the kind of relations that they maintain with the general public and other stakeholders. The act of keeping a sound connection between an association and its public/ representatives/ partners/ financial backers/ investors is known as Public Relations. Communication is a fundamental part in powerful public relations. Two-way correspondence between both the gatherings is fundamental and data should stream in its ideal structure between the association and public. PR is a crucial part of business dealings as they are responsible for the public image of any organisation. Public relations exercises guarantee the right progression of data between the association and its target audience. Public relations go far in keeping up with the brand picture of an association according to its crowd, partners, investors, and all other people who are related with it.

PR is an arranged, supported and assessed process, which through two-way interchange methods, tries to construct commonly useful connections between an association and its public. PR is not only the act of safeguarding but also improving the standing of a specific association/ firm. In modern times, where each association endeavours hard to pursue its image, advertising has turned into a need of great importance. It is fundamental for each association to discuss well with its public/ main interest group.

A professional public relation executive is responsible for making and executing a PR technique, assisting a business or individual with developing a positive standing through different neglected or procured channels and configurations, including press, social media, and in-person commitment.

> "Building a strong team around you and being able to really communicate well with them is part of what's going to bring you a higher level of success."
> -Meghan Markle

Functions & Activities of PR

The functions of a PR are highly dynamic and require public dealing skills and brand building techniques. Following are some of the functions and activities of PR:

1. **Media Relations:** Press coverage is the most common PR activity that helps you reach large customer groups. PR professionals use print or broadcast media to disseminate information about an organisation and its offerings.

2. **Counselling:** Public Relations professionals perform a consulting role by mentoring an organisation's senior management on dedicated communications programmes. They provide suggestions and recommendations on organisational policies and assist in decision-making, especially regarding communications. This helps administrators effectively control the flow of information to the public.

3. **Research:** The associations take on the two-way correspondence models of public relations to work with free progression of data between the association and its public. This aids in utilising exploration and effects the general population and impacts their behaviour.

4. **Press Releases:** These are kind of correspondences which are an official statement by any firm or organisation about the various activities and decisions taken by them. It is meant to give exposure to any activity. It is closely related to media propagation. And is kind of an exposure instrument. Media has a role to play in it as it is often disseminated through print or digital media. In short, a Press Release contains the significant, authentic, and official

activities and day-today functioning of an organisation or a firm are summed up for media dissemination.

5. **Employee Relation:** For an association, its workers are the most crucial and important entities. PR also controls and manages the various internal correspondences like web postings, memos, office orders, note sheets, pamphlets, etc. Also, PR is responsible for efficient and effective client assistance.

6. **Data administration:** PR plays a crucial role in disseminating, storing, and analysing the data that is received in the database of an organisation.

7. **Item Promotion:** PR is equally important in marketing communications as they are the crucial link between an organisation and the public at large.

8. **Relations with Investors:** Shareholders play a very important role in the growth of any organisation as they are the backbone of a solid foundation for the future growth of an organisation. PR executives are known to handle shareholder communications. Shareholders are an essential part of any business organisation and hence a PR executive is the right person to engage with them for the larger interest of the firm.

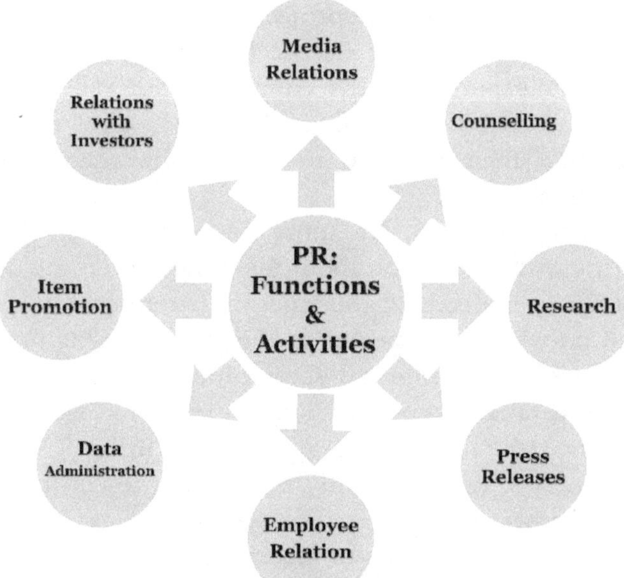

Through the various responsibilities and activities of a PR executive as mentioned above, we can safely assume that the role of a PR is highly dynamic and requires professional skills and an efficient managerial behaviour. It includes almost all aspects of professional communication as enunciated in the diagram above.

Practice
Q1. What is the meaning of Public Relations?
Q2. How does PR function? Explain.

Being an Effective PR

Following are some of the skills that can be incorporated to become an effective PR:

1. **Staying organised.** There is no substitute to organising and prioritising one's work. Proper time management and time distribution can help in being an effective PR as it leads to efficient managerial behaviour in any individual. One ought to distribute time toward the start and end of every day to coordinate the to-do list, assignment list, inbox, and projects.

2. **Communication.** It can be said that a PR should be a communication expert. Effective communication skills enable us to communicate effectively with others. If one is good at communicating their message to others, the chances of error become minimal.

3. **Staying updated:** The more you work in the PR business, the more mindful you will be about the things others are doing. So, it is essential to understand the working patterns of peers and to keep a tab on what is happening in the industry. One needs to be updated about latest events and developments in the industry.

4. **Brand management:** Public relations work includes enhancing the reputation of the organisation's image. One ought to have the option to use the brand's assets and present them in such a way that appeals to the target audience.

5. **Creativity:** PR needs to increase their creativity. Creativity is one of the most crucial skills that need to be developed. This can

be developed by staying updated about industry behaviours and by monitoring the latest developments in the industry. Since every PR situation is different and unique, therefore, one should be creative enough to apply different methodologies while working as a PR. One needs to devise different strategies and methodologies while managing any situation.

6. Setting goals for personal and professional development. Setting goals and endeavouring to achieve them is an effective strategy for improving your skills as a public relations professional. Establishing personal and professional goals will help you measure your progress.

7. **Flexibility:** As a PR specialist, flexibility is one attribute that is central to a successful career in public relations. A PR executive needs to adapt quickly to changing circumstances as each PR situation is unique in itself.

8. **Teamwork:** PR executives should be team-players. One must know the art of administering and disseminating duties so as to get the work done. Teamwork is therefore an essential attribute of any effective PR. One must learn to work in a team. It is important to be able to work well with others in high-pressure situations to carry out effective PR campaigns.

> "Networking is an enrichment program, not an
> entitlement program."
> -Susan Roane

Persuasion Skills

Introducing Persuasion Skills + Aristotle's 3 Modes of Persuasion

The skills of accessing, analysing, evaluating, and creating different types of strategies to communicate in various situations and utilizing major features of language for achieving this goal are known as persuasion skills. There are two prime features of language that are grammatical and content words. Carrying certain meanings for example, nouns, verbs, and adjectives falls under the category of content words. On the other hand, grammatical words serve the purpose of expressing the relationship of words within a sentence that revolve around its function and structure. For example, the way propositions give more informative knowledge regarding nouns, like providing reasons or giving purpose to conjunctions that indicate the relation that ideas and events have with each other. The secret of one's successful personal and professional lives lies in their ability of setting criteria and evaluating their persuasive skills. It has become even more important in today's world of communication networks that have been globalized and our constantly evolving work environment.

The famous Greek philosopher Aristotle gave three modes through which we can persuade. These are *ethos* which means character, *pathos* that stands for emotions and *logos* that means logic and reason. These modes give you the power to shift your audience's mindset from where it is to where you desire it to be.

Ethos is connected to the reliability of the person who speaks or writes, which is reflected through the virtues of one's character, how intelligent they are and the knowledge they have of the subject and their efforts to demonstrate goodwill. It is not necessary for you to have all these qualities but you should have the ability to show these qualities. *Pathos* is the ability to be appealing to your listeners or audience and their emotions such as fear, anger, confidence, patriotism, and kindness. Our way of judgment changes with our emotions like happiness, anger, or fear. The purpose of *Pathos* is to convince your audience through the creation of an emotionally charged response to a story or a plea that is impassioned and can convince. The ability to have arguments with reasons, factual information and examples is known as *Logos*.

> "The triumph of persuasion over force is the sign of a civilized society."
> -Mark Skousen

Importance of Persuasion Skills in Professional Space

Persuasion occurs everywhere. It occurs even in our personal lives and is present in any sort of negotiation or communication. Persuasion skills are dynamic skills which are equally needed in various ways in an official business setting. It can facilitate one's professional lives in various ways.

Some of the ways in which persuasion skills can be useful in a business setting are –

• It is useful in persuading a junior or an intern to perform a particular task.

• To persuade subordinates about a decision made by the management of the company and to take their support.

• It can be used to make your customers buy your services and products.

• To persuade seniors or your management to lend their support in any proposal or initiative

• Persuasion skills can also be useful to guard oneself against any sort of manipulation in a professional setting

> "I think the power of persuasion would be the greatest superpower of all time."
> -Jenny Mollen

How to Improve Persuasion Skills?

Professor Robert B. Cialdini talks about six ways of persuasive skills to influence:

1. Reciprocation

A favour is mostly returned by the majority of the people. Reciprocation is the act of returning something that has been offered to you. It is human nature to have the intention of returning a favour when we are offered something, especially when it is free. This psychological trick can be used for persuasion. Here are a few examples where this trick can work.

- Providing an estimate for free.
- Samples given for free.
- Information that is available for free. Like, leaflets and videos.

These examples tell us how when customers are first given free samples, they feel an obligation to return this favour by buying a product. Similarly, in terms of free information, many creators provide a chunk of an informative video or a course for free and for the full video/ course or its advanced level they have paywalls. Having access to the free information as a demo encourages people to subscribe for the paid information as well.

2. Being committed and consistent

Being committed and consistent to a task or cause conveys a sense of responsibility. When we are committed to something we take up the responsibility to work for that cause and complete it. So, this idea is central to persuasion and can be used to persuade people to contribute to a larger cause. Because when people make a commitment in a written or an oral form to a certain goal or idea, they tend to honour it more. Here are a few examples of how this technique can be applied:

- charities first request people to sign a petition which seems harmless and later they approach people again to make donations.
- when people receive a phone call that asks them if they are going to vote in the upcoming elections, it makes them consistent with voting for other elections as well (in comparison with the people who did not get the phone call).

3. Social proof

Social Proof means a sort of evidence of the benefits of a service or product by the people who have used it. It is one of the most common ways through which we unintentionally advertise a product by talking about its benefits and suggesting others to buy it. For companies it works as a credential of their quality service or product.

This can be used by the companies through giving the example of their satisfied customers to persuade their potential customers to buy and use their products. People are more likely to do the things which they see others doing. Here are some examples of this technique:

- "Have the same experience as the 2000+ people who experienced satisfaction because of the power of…" This phrase can be used to emphasize on the large number of satisfied customers to encourage others to buy your product.
- "Have a look at our 1000 plus happy customers and whose transformations were the results of our skin care products." This shows the reliability of your product to your new customers and makes them think it is worth investing in your product.

> "Persuasion is not a science but an art."
> -William Bernbach

4. A sense of likeness

This refers to the sense of likeness people have towards certain types of people. This can vary from person to person but there is some commonality based on some specific situations. It is common for people to get easily persuaded and convinced by the ones they like. For example-

- Girls as guides are seen as more approachable especially to make the tour more comfortable for women tourists.
- Old folks selling cookies come off as benevolent.

5. Being authoritative

Authoritative people convey a sense of seniority that demands respect and obligates people to listen to them. That is why people in authority are mostly obeyed by people more. This is usually applicable to the people who are senior in terms of their position and experience. For example-

- Dr/ Professors from prestigious universities.

6. Scarcity

Scarcity means shortage. A sense of scarcity is created to boost the sale of a product. It is an age-old formula that companies use by providing limited products in a limited time that generates the need to buy that product urgently before somebody else buys it. When scarcity is perceived, it creates demands.

For example: "Just 1 more left. Avail the discount till midnight"- is one of the most popular phrases that conveys scarcity.

Practice

Q1. What is the significance of Persuasion Skills in professional life?

Q2. What do you understand by Aristotle's 3 modes of persuasion? Explain.

Summary

In this part, we have learned the major components of writing & speaking skills in professional life. Speaking skills play an important role in a professional setting. As part of this part, we learned about the importance of interviews along with their examples and how to prepare for them. Traditionally interviews are conducted in a face-to-face setting. But with the rise of digitalization and its presence in every sphere of our life hence interviews nowadays are held online as well. We also understood some points by which we can improve our interview speaking skills and by which we can learn how to face interviews confidently. Summary & Paraphrase writing are important skills needed in a professional setting. This unit also discussed that.

The relation between a company or organization and its customers/ audience is a crucial one. Here PR plays an important role in building this relationship. We learned about the role of a PR and how it functions along with extensive discussion on how one can be an effective PR. Apart from these skills, Persuasion skills are important professional skills needed in any professional setting. It works at every level so it becomes extremely important to develop this skill. In this part we learned about the significance of persuasion skills and its historical aspects.

At the end of this part, we have learned some major writing skills that play a significant role in one's professional life. Making effective summaries are important in any professional environment to ensure brevity of expression. Paraphrasing too is a much-needed skill which benefits us in almost all professional spheres. We learnt the art of making concise summaries and successful paraphrases.

Within a business sphere it is imperative on the part of employees to create regular reports which may be investigative or analytical in nature. We have learnt how to write both with suitable examples in this section. Also, any professional setting is incomplete without office orders, memos, and minutes of meetings. In this section we understood how to write memos and office orders to highlight important events and information in the office. We also learnt how to note down the minutes of a meeting to ensure credibility and transparency within a professional space.

Then we also understood, through various practical examples, the art of making our own Resume/ CV. We also understood the difference between CV, Bio-Data and a Resume. Through multiple examples we understood how CV writing can be made more effective. By practicing the various intext questions provided, the students can gain even better hands-on knowledge and training in honing their written skills within professional settings.

Glossary

Beating Around the Bush: It is an idiom which means to avoid or delay answering a question or coming to your main point while continuing to talk about other related but unimportant things.

Brevity: Concise and exact use of words while writing.

Business Communication: The communication that takes place within a professional space or workplace is called Business Communication.

Buzzword: Any word which creates news and is used at any particular time, e.g., FOMO (fear of missing out), Deep Dive (means brainstorming), etc.

Capsule Summaries: It is a way of denoting a very brief short summary of anything and to denote anything which is short and concise.

Comprehension Skills: Set of skills which allow one to comprehend or understand something. Comprehension skills include reading, skimming, analysing, summarizing, inferencing etc. Together they allow a reader to construct meaning out of a text.

Crux: Most important point or the essence of something.

Digital Communication: A form of communication established through the digital or online mode and not in person or manually written form. For example, communication through email, text messages or voicemail.

Hashtags: Hashtag is symbolized by a hash (#) symbol. It is used in the context of social media for using keywords associated with your post that helps in finding the interested audience for your topic or post and vice-versa.

Information Overload: This means putting too much information which defeats the purpose of effective communication. This leads to problem of plenty.

Interviewee: In an interview setting, the person who is being asked questions and answers them is known as interviewee. Interviewee is the person who has applied for a job and is being interviewed in a job interview.

Interviewer: When an interview is taking place, the person who asks the questions and takes the interview of someone is called an interviewer, especially in job interviews.

LinkedIn profile URL: URL means Uniform Resource Locator which is a unique address of any link on the internet. In case of LinkedIn mostly the URL is something like – https://www.linkedin.com/in/tannu247alka

Redundant: Superfluous, unnecessary, repetitive.

Skype, G-Meet, MS Teams: These are some mobile and computer-based video calling applications. They are mostly used for professional purposes like business meetings, online classes, and other forms of digital correspondences etc. Though they were used in various professional settings, their usage in everyday and professional life has increased manifold in the post covid-19 pandemic era.

Social Media Etiquettes: Etiquettes to follow while using social media or the rightful behaviour on social media to avoid being offensive to others.

Standardization: The act of establishing a standard, assigning certain qualities to something that become its characteristics.

SWOT Analysis: It is an acronym for "Strength, Weakness, Opportunity, Threat". This is a strategy planning technique in which you are supposed to make a list of your company's strengths, weaknesses, its opportunities, and threats. It helps you analyse the situation and find its solution. In the context of a job interview, it is meant to quickly remember the key aspects of your qualities of analysis, management and planning when asked.

Tweeting: Here Tweeting is used in the context of social media. The act of making a post on social media app 'Twitter', nowadays known as X, is known as Tweeting.

USP: It is an acronym for "Unique Selling Point" or "Unique Selling Proposition". It means someone's unique quality that sets them apart from their competitors. In professional life and especially in the context of job interviews, employees ask this to filter out the candidates based on their USP that best serves their job requirements.

Self-Assessment Questions

1. From what you have learned in the module, prepare an interview of your choice and make comments on it while focusing on the answers of the interviewee.

2. Explain how an online interview is different from a face-to-face interview and what are the key steps to prepare for an online interview.

3. Explain the significance of PR in professional life and how you can be effective at it.

4. What is the role of speaking skills in the functioning and effectiveness of a PR? Elaborate.

5. Referring to Robert B. Cialdini's 6 ways of Persuasion, explain your own understanding of different ways of persuasion with examples.

6. Share your views on how persuasion can be used in everyday life and expand your views on its use in professional settings.

7. Digital Communications in professional lives is now taking a centre stage in almost all spheres of professional lives. Elaborate.

8. Write your own CV following the lines of the various examples shared earlier. It should be detailed and comprehensive. Your CV should contain your education and career history, positions held, academic projects, skills, participation in any co-curricular activities, achievements, etc.

9. Imagine you have a degree in graphic designing from a reputed university. Write a job application letter to a company which works in the field of professional designing with an aim to look for a job in your field. Enquire about any vacancies that may have arisen in the company for you.

10. Mr. AK Sharma is working at Keynes Logistics Pvt. Ltd. as an Assistant Secretary, Sales Department since the past 10 years. He has to apply for the post of Joint Director, Kriyansh Logistical Care Pvt. Ltd. as he is looking to shift his job for a better career opportunity. Create a brief job-application letter for him in this regard.

11. Enumerate some basic etiquettes that are required while using Twitter.

12. Read any book of your choice. Prepare a book review in 300-400 words on it. It can be a fiction/ non-fiction/ autobiography/ a book of poetry/ self-help book, or any other book of your choice.

13. Create your own personal blog on any blog site provider. What are the ways in which you can increase the number of visitors on your blog?

14. What is LinkedIn? Discuss some basic points that need to be kept in mind while creating a LinkedIn profile.

15. Create your own LinkedIn profile taking help from the points discussed in the study material.

16. What are the key differences between a summary and a paraphrase?

17. Search for any comprehension passage of your choice from any online source. Attempt a summary of the same keeping in mind the points discussed above in the study material.

18. Search for any comprehension passage of your choice from any online source. Attempt a paraphrase of the same keeping in mind the points discussed above in the study material.

19. To honour the 79th Independence Day, Union Cabinet Ministry of Parliamentary Affairs has celebrated nationalist and patriotic events bimonthly for one full year. As the social media head of this ministry, draft an extensive report, highlighting the various historic events which have happened over the last one year. You have to submit this report to the office of the President & Vice-President. Prepare a detailed report.

20. Recently, there has been some cases of food-poisoning in the canteen of Delhi College of Finance located in New Delhi. As food inspector you have been asked by your officer-in-charge to probe the event in depth and submit a report of the findings within a fortnight. Draft an investigative report for the same. Also, offer your recommendations and suggestions.

21. What is the main difference between a Memo Report & Letter Report?

22. What is the difference between Memos & Office Orders?

References

Garg, Manoj Kumar (2019). *English Communication: Theory & Practice*. New Delhi. Scholar Tech Press.

Cialdini, Robert B. (1993). *Influence: The Psychology of Persuasion*. New York, Harper Collins Publishers.

Suggested Readings

Campbell, Devay (2015). *The Best Job Interview Advice Book*. United States of America, Career Cents.

Choudhury, S. K., Dev, A. N., Mathur, A., Prasad, T., & Shahnaaz, T. (2008). *Business English: Department of English*. Pearson Longman.

Spiropoulos, Michael (2005). *Interview Skills that Win the Job: Simple Techniques for Answering all the Tough Questions*. Australia, McPherson.

Sweeney, Simon (2004). *Communicating in Business*. Cambridge University Press.

Sweeney, Simon (2003). *English for Business Communication*. Cambridge University Press.

Choudhury, S. K., Dev, A. N., Mathur, A., Prasad, T., & Shahnaaz, T. (2008). *Business English*. Department of English, University of Delhi. Pearson Longman.

Hazarika, Breez Mohan., Chetia, Kironmoy., & Bania, Pranami (2019). *Interface: A Textbook for AECC English Communication*. New Delhi. Worldview Publications.

Macarthy, Andrew (2015). *500 Social Media Marketing Tips: Essential Advice, Hints and Strategy for Business: Facebook, Twitter, Pinterest, Google+, YouTube, Instagram, LinkedIn, and More!*

McGee, Paul (2009). *How to Write a CV that Really Works*, Devon. How to Content.

Spiropoulos, Michael (2005). *Interview Skills that Win the Job*, Allen & Unwin.

Corfield, Rebecca (2009*). Preparing the Perfect Job Application: Application Forms and Letters Made Easy*, London. Kogan Page Limited.

Bowden, John (2004). *Writing a Report: How to Prepare, Write and Present Effective Reports*, Devon UK. How to Content.

Moon, Jon (2007). *How to Make an Impact: Influence, Inform & Impress with your Reports, Presentations, Business Documents*. Edinburgh. Pearson Education.

PRAISE FOR THE BOOK

Communication is the core foundation that connects communities, cultures, societies, and nations. It contributes to mutual understanding and valuing, thereby building and consolidating groups, and communities. What brings the entire human race together is our ability to express and connect. The book *The Art of Professional Communication: Strategies for Success in Professional Life* is intended to appeal to readers traversing cultures. The author has delved into the complexities of professional life, and through a variety of examples, he has elucidated the multifarious ways in which one can strategize and communicate better.

In its emphasis on practical applications and contemporary relevance, the book is different from the traditional textbooks on the subject. It is a valuable learning tool that is intended to equip the readers with the vital skills needed for real-world success. In addition, with socially relevant topics like the role of cultural factors in communication; this book provisions a step-by-step guide to build and consolidate communities and professional ties across cultures and nations.

The personalized quotes embedded throughout the book offer instances of inspiration, encouraging students to think critically and perceive the broader implications of effective communication. Closely adhering to the NEP-2020 curriculum, this book is tailored for university students and offers to them the roadmap to master the art of professional communication. For students seeking to excel in their studies and careers, this book is an indispensable companion.

Prof. Neera Agnimitra
Chairperson, International Relations, University of Delhi
Professor, Department of Social Work, Delhi School of Social Work
University of Delhi

Prof. Neera Agnimitra is Sr. Professor with over 35 years of teaching experience. She is also the Chairperson, Governing Body, Vivekananda College, University of Delhi. She is an administrator, social worker and an expert member on many committees constituted by government and non-government bodies. She also figures on the editorial boards of many national and international journals and is a reviewer for several renowned publishing houses including Sage, Springer, Oxford, Elsevier, and Routledge.

The Sanskrit term Saṃpreṣaṇa (संप्रेषण or communication) offers profound insight into the rich heritage of communication in ancient India. In ancient Bhārata, Saṃpreṣaṇa was not just about conveying information but also about transmitting knowledge, wisdom, culture, and values. Bhārata had theoretical modes of Saṃpreṣaṇa since millennia. The most basic way this tradition thrived in ancient Bhārata was through Śruti (Heard) & Smṛti (Remembered). Apart from these verbal aspects, there are certain non-verbal aspects too which the ancient Bhāratīya traditions touched upon like Mudrā (symbolic gestures), Abhinayā (facial expressions), Namastē (greetings), and several others. All these aspects of body language played a profound role in communicating not just between individuals but with the divine, the self, and the universe. There is an extant and enduring tradition still associated with Saṃpreṣaṇa in Bhāratīya culture even today.

Bhārata today stands at a defining moment when the youth of our country is poised to bring Bhārata to the centre stage and bring the cultural and professional prowess of the nation to the whole world. I am sure, the present book *The Art of Professional Communication: Strategies for Success in Professional Life* aims to do this and will help youth embarking on their professional life.

Communication is basic to human interactions. What is perhaps equally basic is to derive pleasure out of words and communication. As the saying goes: हितं मनोहारि च दुर्लभं वचः।। which gets translated as "Words that are beneficial & pleasing to the mind, are rare to find" therefore, all our modes of communication must be aimed towards pleasant modes of expression. The ancient text *Hitopadeśa* mentions the power of speech in communication: शास्त्रं शस्त्रं च करुणा वागेव साधनं परम्। सर्वं श्रुतं च भाषणं धर्मं वा हितमात्मनः ।। which gets translated as "Among all weapons and scriptures, speech is the ultimate tool. Words heard and spoken with wisdom lead to righteousness and benefit the self." The current book aims to bring wisdom to the readers who are embarking on their journey of professional life by allowing the readers to use correct modes of expression in their workplace and in their professional journey. I wish all the best to the author & to the readers.

Prof. Ranjan K. Tripathi
Dean, Students' Welfare, University of Delhi
Professor, Department of Sanskrit, University of Delhi

Prof. Ranjan Kumar Tripathi, an able administrator, researcher, and social worker has published dozens of books & research papers. His areas of interest include Sanskrit poetics. He is the recipient of numerous honours, including Akhil Bhartiya Vidvat Parishad, Varanasi,

2016; Vikram Kalidasa Award, MP Govt, 2016; Rashtriya Utkrisht Kshatra Samman from Shiksha Vibhag of Ministry of HRD, 1998.

The Art of Professional Communication: Strategies for Success in Professional Life focuses on the skills, strategy and art of communication which makes it a perfect guide for the students of communication courses and readers who wish to improve their communication skills. Communication as a concept is the first step towards enlightenment. The book stays true to the motto of Hansraj College, "तमसो मा ज्योतिर्गमय" which means "lead me from darkness to light". It indeed is a handbook which leads the path towards light, out of darkness & will prove to be indispensable for students pursuing their professional careers. It gives me immense pleasure to see that my junior colleague at Hansraj College, one of the North Nodal Cluster Colleges of University of Delhi, has come up with this book based closely on skill enhancement and practical training for university going students. I believe this book will prove to be their guide to master the art of communication. I heartily congratulate the author for his invaluable contribution for the students with this book. Best of luck to the author and the readers!

Prof. Rama
Principal, Hansraj College,
University of Delhi

Prof. (Dr.) Rama is Principal, Hansraj College, University of Delhi which is one of the largest constituent colleges of DU. She is the first female Principal of the 77-year-old college and has held the position since 2015. She has authored more than 30 books on media, communication & literature. As a critic, journalist & media personality, she has a teaching experience of more than 30 years at the University of Delhi.

The title of this book *The Art of Professional Communication: Strategies for Success in Professional Life* juxtaposes two very important and seemingly contrasting elements – 'art' and 'strategies'. In popular understanding, art is associated with spontaneity, creativity, and inherent abilities/ talent. It is seldom seen as something that needs to be strategized. However, anyone who is creative can tell you that while there may be instances of art being the outcome of talent, it is not hundred percent creativity – it involves a fair amount of perspiration!

It took John Keats months to come up with what seems like a really simple line – "A thing of Beauty/ Is a joy forever." Simplicity cannot take away from the effectiveness of this line but Keats worked hard to achieve this. Art has to be strategized. That is why, we 'teach' creative writing! or painting! and so on. For each genre, the tools are different. While creative writing may make use of figures of speech, painting or sculpture is a totally different ball game. And then there are sub-genres. Picasso learnt traditional art and only when he felt he had mastered it, did he experiment and come up with what we call 'modern art'.

The book *The Art of Professional Communication: Strategies for Success in Professional Life* underlines the fact that in the professional world, to be able to make an impact, one has to be an able communicator and have the dexterity to utilize all channels of communication that are nowadays available. The personal, the social and the professional have in a certain sense, merged. Hence, it is not only for personal and social reasons that one uses Twitter or Instagram or Facebook; one uses it for professional reasons like networking and projection. Hence, it is only appropriate that we use it responsibly, ethically, and of course effectually.

So, the author addresses all these modes of communication, be it traditional forms like letters/ emails and the more contemporary forms of social media channels and handholds the reader as to how these can be used successfully. The book is a ready handbook and a step-by-step guide for communication. It could be a great go-to book for anyone who wishes to be a skilled communicator.

Prof. Swati Pal
Principal, Janki Devi Memorial College, University of Delhi
Fulbright-Nehru International Education Administrator 2024-25

Swati Pal, Professor and Principal, Janki Devi Memorial College, is a Fullbright-Nehru Fellowship Scholar, a Charles Wallace Scholar and the first Asian Scholar to receive the John McGrath Theatre Studies Scholarship at Edinburgh University. Author of several books on theatre, creative and academic writing, she also writes poetry and is the Vice-Chair at the Indian Association for Commonwealth Literature and Language Studies.

The Art of Professional Communication: Strategies for Success in Professional Life is a valuable handbook for both students and professionals. A practical approach sets this book apart from several others available as it seeks to enhance communication in the professional sphere. Catering to the Skill

Enhancement Course prescribed under the UGCF-2022 as part of the New Education Policy-2020, this book has a greater focus on practical aspects of communication. It is relevant in the contemporary scenario of fast-moving changes in the dynamic professional space.

From physical letters to online blogs, from etiquettes in the professional space to netiquettes, from writing book reviews to writing for twitter, it has covered all aspects of modern-day communication. Concisely written in lucid language, the self-assessment tasks are an additional bonus as it helps the learners pace themselves as they engage in self-practice. The summary at the end of every chapter reinforces key concepts and personalized quotes give a larger perspective. I recommend this insightful book on communication to both students and professionals.

Prof. Gitanjali Chawla
Department of English, Maharaja Agrasen College
University of Delhi

Prof. Gitanjali Chawla, has more than thirty years of teaching experience at Maharaja Agrasen College, University of Delhi. A long-time editor of Fortell, she is currently its Vice President and has also been the Presidential International Visiting Scholar at Boston University, Boston, USA.

Communication skills are the skills of the 21st century. It is an emerging life skill. This idea is materialised in NEP-2020 and in the syllabi of University of Delhi, which envisages imparting life skills and professional skills as part of holistic education. This book incorporates the core thrust of the NEP i.e., the idea of communication as reflected in the wide range of SEC courses that DU offers. Since, now all the major universities of India are implementing the NEP-2020, the book will be useful for young students entering the world of professional communication for the first time.

Communication is entrenched in the education policy and this book captures its essence thoroughly. Apart from core professional communication skills, several other topics like Netiquettes, Public Relations, Negotiations and Persuasion skills are extremely dynamic skills of the 21st century which the book also addresses and covers in minute details. Each chapter of the book feels like a carefully drawn map, revealing the hidden currents, and shifting tides of professional life, allowing readers to sail smoothly through challenges that may otherwise seem daunting. The book does more than just teach—it engages, inviting students to not only learn but to also reflect.

As the quote by Irish poet and playwright W.B. Yeats goes: "Think like a wise man but communicate in the language of the people", similarly, the book *The Art of Professional Communication: Strategies for Success in Professional Life* explains concepts and ideas in a cogent and lucid manner and makes the entire exercise of reading a book on communication extremely pleasurable. This book not only meets academic expectations but exceeds them, offering itself as a treasure chest of knowledge for those wise enough to open it. For students seeking to master the art of professional communication, this book is not just a recommendation—it is a revelation.

Dr. Animesh Naskar

Member, Academic Panel, Office of Dean Academics, University of
Delhi
Associate Professor, Department of Economics
Hansraj College, University of Delhi

Dr. Animesh Naskar is an academician, researcher and administrator who was the former Joint Dean, Academic Affairs, University of Delhi. He is also a Visiting Faculty at Lal Bahadur Shastri Institute of Management, 2021. He is a recipient of several research scholarships & also a recipient of Delhi University Faculty Development Programme Scholarship in 2012.

ACKNOWLEDGEMENTS

Writing acknowledgements is a tricky affair as the creation of this book was not done in isolation. I am deeply grateful to all those who have contributed to the creation of this book. Their support has been invaluable throughout this journey. First and foremost, I would like to thank my family who has stood by me all these years that I was in the elaborate process of writing this book. Their constant encouragement helped me give my best & it is because of them that this book saw the light of the day.

I would also like to acknowledge Mr. Anuj Kumar, Founder & Publisher, Kalamos Literary Services for his meticulous editing, thoughtful feedback and professional outlook. Most importantly, I wish to thank him for his inordinate patience which gave me the hope to complete this monumental task despite several delays. His positive outlook & commitment to excellence has been instrumental in bringing this book to fruition.

I extend my warm appreciation to my colleagues and peers who provided valuable insights and feedback during various discussions that I had with them. Their perspectives have been instrumental in shaping the direction of this work and increasing the practical relevance of this book. I thank my friends for their unwavering support, patience, and understanding throughout this endeavor. From constructive feedback to proof reading, the encouragement I have received from them helped me persist during the challenges and inspired me to strive for quality and excellence throughout the course of writing this book. I humbly and wholeheartedly acknowledge your support and I can say with absolute certainty that this book would not have been possible without you. I owe a lot to my peers and friends. To many other who have supported me behind the scenes, thank you for your contributions, encouragement, and belief in this project.

<u>NOTES</u>